Writing 2

A Revised Edition of
Reflection and Beyond

• •

Meredith Pike-Baky

Laurie Blass

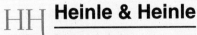
Heinle & Heinle
Thomson Learning™

Australia • Canada • Denmark • Japan • Mexico
New Zealand • Philippines • Puerto Rico • Singapore
Spain • United Kingdom • United States

Developmental Editors: Jennifer Monaghan, Jill Korey O'Sullivan
Sr. Production Coordinator: Maryellen E. Killeen
Market Development Director: Charlotte Sturdy
Sr. Manufacturing Coordinator: Mary Beth Hennebury
Interior Design: Julia Gecha
Illustrations: Pre-Press Company, Inc., Antonio Castro
Photo Research: Martha Friedman

Cover Design: Ha Nguyen Design
Cover Images: PhotoDisc®
Composition/Production: Pre-Press Company, Inc.
Freelance Production Editor: Janet McCartney
Copyeditor: Donald Pharr
Printer/Binder: Bawden

For permission to use material from this text, contact us:
web   www.thomsonrights.com
fax   1-800-730-2215
phone   1-800-730-2214

For photo credits, see page 237.

Heinle & Heinle Publishers
20 Park Plaza
Boston, MA 02116

UK/EUROPE/MIDDLE EAST:
Thomson Learning
Berkshire House
168-173 High Holborn
London, WC1V 7AA, United Kingdom

AUSTRALIA/NEW ZEALAND:
Nelson/Thomson Learning
102 Dodds Street
South Melbourne
Victoria 3205 Australia

CANADA:
Nelson/Thomson Learning
1120 Birchmount Road
Scarborough, Ontario
Canada M1K 5G4

LATIN AMERICA:
Thomson Learning
Seneca, 53
Colonia Polanco
11560 México D.F. México

ASIA (excluding Japan):
Thomson Learning
60 Albert Street #15-01
Albert Complex
Singapore 189969

JAPAN:
Thomson Learning
Palaceside Building, 5F
1-1-1 Hitotsubashi, Chiyoda-ku
Tokyo 100 0003, Japan

SPAIN:
Thomson Learning
Calle Magallanes, 25
28015-Madrid
España

Library of Congress Cataloging-in-Publication Data
Blass, Laurie
    Tapestry writing 2 / Meredith Pike-Baky, Laurie Blass.
       p. cm.
    ISBN 0-8384-0038-8 (alk. paper)
    1. English language—Textbooks for foreign speakers. 2. English
language—Rhetoric—Problems, exercises, etc. 3. Report writing—Problems, exercises,
etc. I. Title: Tapestry writing two. II. Pike-Baky, Meredith, – III. Title.

PE1128 .B5927 2000
808'.042—dc21   99-089165

This book is printed on acid-free recycled paper.

Printed in the United States of America.
1 2 3 4 5 6 7 8 9 03 02 01 00

A VERY SPECIAL THANK YOU

The publisher and authors would like to thank the following coordinators and instructors who have offered many helpful insights and suggestions for change throughout the development of the new *Tapestry*.

Alicia Aguirre, *Cañada College*
Fred Allen, *Mission College*
Maya Alvarez-Galvan, *University of Southern California*
Geraldine Arbach, *Collège de l'Outaouais, Canada*
Dolores Avila, *Pasadena City College*
Sarah Bain, *Eastern Washington University*
Kate Baldus, *San Francisco State University*
Fe Baran, *Chabot College*
Gail Barta, *West Valley College*
Karen Bauman, *Biola University*
Liza Becker, *Mt. San Antonio College*
Leslie Biaggi, *Miami-Dade Community College*
Andrzej Bojarczak, *Pasadena City College*
Nancy Boyer, *Golden West College*
Glenda Bro, *Mt. San Antonio College*
Brooke Brummitt, *Palomar College*
Linda Caputo, *California State University, Fresno*
Alyce Campbell, *Mt. San Antonio College*
Barbara Campbell, *State University of New York, Buffalo*
Robin Carlson, *Cañada College*
Ellen Clegg, *Chapman College*
Karin Cintron, *Aspect ILS*
Diane Colvin, *Orange Coast College*
Martha Compton, *University of California, Irvine*
Nora Dawkins, *Miami-Dade Community College*
Beth Erickson, *University of California, Davis*
Charles Estus, *Eastern Michigan University*
Gail Feinstein Forman, *San Diego City College*
Jeffra Flaitz, *University of South Florida*
Kathleen Flynn, *Glendale Community College*
Ann Fontanella, *City College of San Francisco*
Sally Gearhart, *Santa Rosa Junior College*
Alice Gosak, *San José City College*
Kristina Grey, *Northern Virginia Community College*
Tammy Guy, *University of Washington*
Gail Hamilton, *Hunter College*
Patty Heiser, *University of Washington*
Virginia Heringer, *Pasadena City College*

Catherine Hirsch, *Mt. San Antonio College*
Helen Huntley, *West Virginia University*
Nina Ito, *California State University, Long Beach*
Patricia Jody, *University of South Florida*
Diana Jones, *Angloamericano, Mexico*
Loretta Joseph, *Irvine Valley College*
Christine Kawamura, *California State University, Long Beach*
Gregory Keech, *City College of San Francisco*
Kathleen Keesler, *Orange Coast College*
Daryl Kinney, *Los Angeles City College*
Maria Lerma, *Orange Coast College*
Mary March, *San José State University*
Heather McIntosh, *University of British Columbia, Canada*
Myra Medina, *Miami-Dade Community College*
Elizabeth Mejia, *Washington State University*
Cristi Mitchell, *Miami-Dade Community College*
Sylvette Morin, *Orange Coast College*
Blanca Moss, *El Paso Community College*
Karen O'Neill, *San José State University*
Bjarne Nielsen, *Central Piedmont Community College*
Katy Ordon, *Mission College*
Luis Quesada, *Miami-Dade Community College*
Gustavo Ramírez Toledo, *Colegio Cristóbol Colón, Mexico*
Nuha Salibi, *Orange Coast College*
Alice Savage, *North Harris College*
Dawn Schmid, *California State University, San Marcos*
Mary Kay Seales, *University of Washington*
Denise Selleck, *City College of San Francisco*
Gail Slater, *Brooklyn and Staten Island Superintendency*
Susanne Spangler, *East Los Angeles College*
Karen Stanley, *Central Piedmont Community College*
Sara Storm, *Orange Coast College*
Margaret Teske, *ELS Language Centers*
Maria Vargas-O'Neel, *Miami-Dade Community College*
James Wilson, *Mt. San Antonio College and Pasadena City College*
Karen Yoshihara, *Foothill College*

ACKNOWLEDGMENTS

Special thanks to these students who made valuable contributions to the revision of this book: Margarita Esponda, Ming-Che Wu, Sandy Ling-Yin Wei, Kevin Lam, Jennifer Liu, Carol Chen, Anne Chen-Han Li, Kyoko Sakata, Prior Huang, Elizabeth Yu-Pin Sheng, Laura Boulet, Ana Paula Issa Kimura, Hiroyuki Matsumaru, and JooHee Cho.

Tapestry Writing 2: Contents

![Academic Power Strategies icon] ACADEMIC POWER STRATEGIES	![CNN icon] CNN VIDEO CLIPS	GRAMMAR YOU CAN USE	FROM READING TO WRITING
Find the place where you do your best work.	"Hollywood Manicurist" The story of a retired Hollywood manicurist who worked with the great movie stars.	Past and past habitual verb tenses	Reading 1: a story in which a woman recalls a time in her childhood when she did something naughty Reading 2: a selection in which a man remembers his childhood impressions of his father's most treasured possessions from China **Writing Activity:** A narrative of an unforgettable event from your past
Find a mentor to help you in and out of school.	"Coach, Teacher, Friend" A profile of a coach and teacher admired by his community for the difference he has made in the lives of his students.	Past perfect tense	Reading 1: a selection in which the writer speaks of the aunt she admired in her childhood Reading 2: a selection in which the writer reflects on the life her mother led before getting married and having children **Writing Activity:** A description of a person you admire
Learn the names of your classmates, teachers, and important people on campus and in your community.	"Married Names" A look at choices made by women to keep or change their names after marriage.	Passive voice	Reading 1: an article about non-traditional naming options for children Reading 2: two selections by people with unusual names **Writing Activity:** An explanation of the meaning, origin, associations, and advantages/disadvantages of your name
Explore learning resources on campus.	"Learning at Home" A report on the advantages and disadvantages of home schooling.	Using *make* and *do* correctly	Reading 1: a book excerpt about the relationship between culture and learning styles Reading 2: a textbook excerpt about the different kinds of learning styles **Writing Activity:** An essay explaining and justifying your learning style
Keep a journal to connect your personal life to school assignments.	"Hawaiian Petroglyphs" A look at a place of special archeological interest in Hawaii.	Result clauses: *so* + adjective (*that*)	Reading 1: a book excerpt in which the author describes one of her favorite places Reading 2: an excerpt from a magazine article about recent changes made to Grand Central Station in New York City **Writing Activity:** A descriptive essay about a place that creates a strong feeling in you

CHAPTER	WRITING SKILLS FOCUS	LANGUAGE LEARNING STRATEGIES
6 **Musical Ambassadors** Page 124 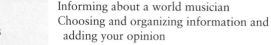 	Informing about a world musician Choosing and organizing information and adding your opinion	Listen to music to improve your English. Group new words and ideas into categories.
7 **Let's Party!** Page 146	Describing a celebration Looking for words and expressions in reading passages that you can use in your own writing Studying how other writers organize ideas	When you read, look for words and expressions that you can use in your writing. Study how other writers organize ideas.
8 **Great Classic Movies** Page 170	Evaluating and summarizing movies Studying noun suffixes to expand your writing vocabulary Taking notes to prepare for a writing assignment Reading an English-language newspaper or magazine at least once a week to improve your writing	Identify your learning goals before you begin a new lesson. Read an English-language newspaper or magazine at least once a week to make your writing more fluent.
9 **Highlights of the Twentieth Century** Page 190 	Describing and evaluating an important person or event Filling in a chart as you brainstorm for ideas for your writing Choosing a writing topic that interests you Using a variety of sources for supporting information	Use a variety of sources when you need facts, examples, details, or statistics to support your ideas in writing. Fill in a chart as you brainstorm for ideas for your writing.
10 **Looking Forward** Page 212 	Predicting a technological product or service of the future Identifying main ideas for reading and writing Creating an outline to organize your ideas before you begin writing	Identify the main idea of a reading passage. Create an outline to organize your ideas before you begin writing.

ACADEMIC POWER STRATEGIES	CNN VIDEO CLIPS	GRAMMAR YOU CAN USE	FROM READING TO WRITING
Use the television as a learning tool.	"Angelique Kidjo" An interview with Angelique Kidjo, a singer from West Africa.	Sentence combining with *not only . . . , but also*	Reading 1: a newspaper article about Yanni, a musician from Greece Reading 2: an article from a web site about Angelique Kidjo, a musician from West Africa **Writing Activity:** An informative essay about one or two musicians you admire or want to learn more about
Study with a partner to help make you a better student and help you enjoy school more.	"Costumes at Carnival" A look at the annual winter Carnival in Venice, Italy.	Phrasal verbs	Reading 1: an interview in which five people tell about their favorite celebrations Reading 2: a newspaper article about a special New Year celebration **Writing Activity:** A descriptive essay about a celebration you are familiar with or one you would like to learn more about
Take good notes on information that you watch or read in preparation for writing.	"A Scene from a Different Kind of Classic Movie" A profile of Oscar Micheaux, an African American movie producer from the past.	Time clauses with *while*	Reading 1: an interview in which four people speak about their favorite movies Reading 2: a review of the movie, *The Wizard of Oz* **Writing Activity:** A summary and evaluation of a movie
Choose what interests you the most whenever you have a choice of assignments.	"Stamps of the Century" A look at United States Postal Service stamps that reflect important people and events of the twentieth century.	Review of past forms Cause and result expressions	Reading 1: an article about one of the most famous singers of the twentieth century, Elvis Presley Reading 2: an article about one of the most important events of the twentieth century, the discovery of DNA **Writing Activity:** An essay about an important person or event of the twentieth century
Learn to manage your time as you move forward in your studies.	"Future Technology" A futurist talks about future technology.	Future expressions Using gerunds to explain how something works	Reading 1: a magazine article about an online virtual hospital Reading 2: a magazine article about a new kind of Internet-linked, interactive television **Writing Activity:** An essay predicting a technological product or service of the future

Welcome to TAPESTRY!

Empower your students with the Tapestry Writing series!

Language learning can be seen as an ever-developing tapestry woven with many threads and colors. The elements of the tapestry are related to different language skills such as listening and speaking, reading, and writing; the characteristics of the teachers; the desires, needs, and backgrounds of the students; and the general second language development process. When all of these elements are working together harmoniously, the result is a colorful, continuously growing tapestry of language competence of which the student and the teacher can be proud.

Tapestry is built upon a framework of concepts that helps students become proficient in English and prepared for the academic and social challenges in college and beyond. The following principles underlie the instruction provided in all of the components of the **Tapestry** program:

- Empowering students to be responsible for their learning
- Using Language Learning Strategies and Academic Power Strategies to enhance one's learning, both in and out of the classroom
- Offering motivating activities that recognize a variety of learning styles
- Providing authentic and meaningful input to heighten learning and communication
- Learning to understand and value different cultures
- Integrating language skills to increase communicative competence
- Providing goals and ongoing self-assessment to monitor progress

Guide to Tapestry Writing

Setting Goals focuses students' attention on the learning they will do in each chapter.

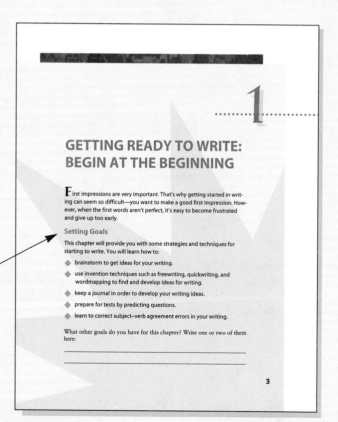

GETTING READY TO WRITE: BEGIN AT THE BEGINNING

First impressions are very important. That's why getting started in writing can seem so difficult—you want to make a good first impression. However, when the first words aren't perfect, it's easy to become frustrated and give up too early.

Setting Goals

This chapter will provide you with some strategies and techniques for starting to write. You will learn how to:

- brainstorm to get ideas for your writing.
- use invention techniques such as freewriting, quickwriting, and wordmapping to find and develop ideas for writing.
- keep a journal in order to develop your writing ideas.
- prepare for tests by predicting questions.
- learn to correct subject–verb agreement errors in your writing.

What other goals do you have for this chapter? Write one or two of them here:

_____

_____

3

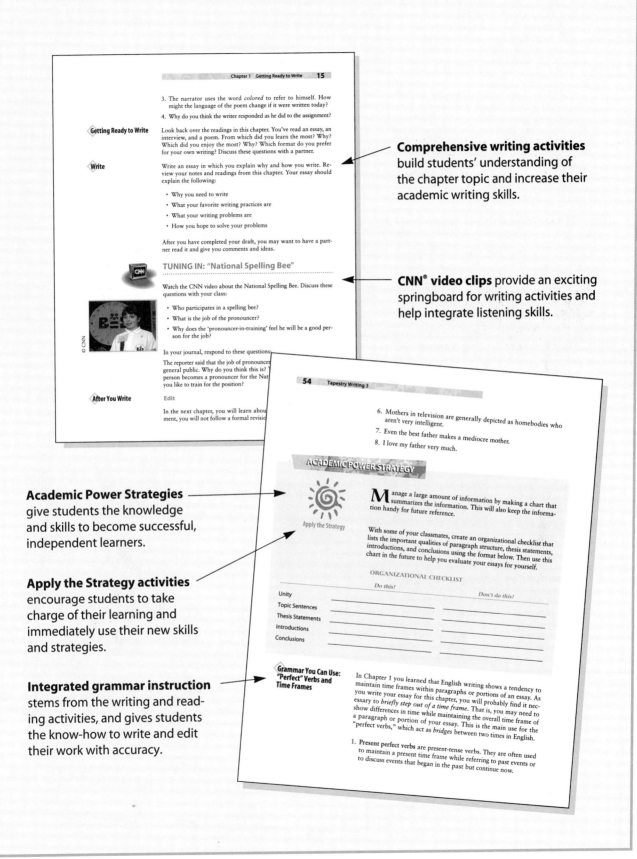

3. The narrator uses the word *colored* to refer to himself. How might the language of the poem change if it were written today?

4. Why do you think the writer responded as he did to the assignment?

◆ **Getting Ready to Write**

Look back over the readings in this chapter. You've read an essay, an interview, and a poem. From which did you learn the most? Why? Which did you enjoy the most? Why? Which format do you prefer for your own writing? Discuss these questions with a partner.

◆ **Write**

Write an essay in which you explain why and how you write. Review your notes and readings from this chapter. Your essay should explain the following:

- Why you need to write
- What your favorite writing practices are
- What your writing problems are
- How you hope to solve your problems

After you have completed your draft, you may want to have a partner read it and give you comments and ideas.

TUNING IN: "National Spelling Bee"

Watch the CNN video about the National Spelling Bee. Discuss these questions with your class:

- Who participates in a spelling bee?
- What is the job of the pronouncer?
- Why does the 'pronouncer-in-training' feel he will be a good person for the job?

In your journal, respond to these questions:

The reporter said that the job of pronoun[cer]... general public. Why do you think this is? ... person becomes a pronouncer for the Nat[ional]... you like to train for the position?

◆ **After You Write**   Edit

In the next chapter, you will learn abou[t]... ment, you will not follow a formal revisi[on]...

Comprehensive writing activities build students' understanding of the chapter topic and increase their academic writing skills.

CNN® video clips provide an exciting springboard for writing activities and help integrate listening skills.

---

6. Mothers in television are generally depicted as homebodies who aren't very intelligent.

7. Even the best father makes a mediocre mother.

8. I love my father very much.

ACADEMIC POWER STRATEGY

Apply the Strategy

Manage a large amount of information by making a chart that summarizes the information. This will also keep the information handy for future reference.

With some of your classmates, create an organizational checklist that lists the important qualities of paragraph structure, thesis statements, introductions, and conclusions using the format below. Then use this chart in the future to help you evaluate your essays for yourself.

ORGANIZATIONAL CHECKLIST

	Do this!	Don't do this!
Unity		
Topic Sentences		
Thesis Statements		
Introductions		
Conclusions		

◆ **Grammar You Can Use: "Perfect" Verbs and Time Frames**

In Chapter 1 you learned that English writing shows a tendency to maintain time frames within paragraphs or portions of an essay. As you write your essay for this chapter, you will probably find it necessary to *briefly step out of a time frame.* That is, you may need to show differences in time while maintaining the overall time frame of a paragraph or portion of your essay. This is the main use for the "perfect verbs," which act as *bridges* between two times in English.

1. **Present perfect verbs** are present-tense verbs. They are often used to maintain a present time frame while referring to past events or to discuss events that began in the past but continue now.

Academic Power Strategies give students the knowledge and skills to become successful, independent learners.

Apply the Strategy activities encourage students to take charge of their learning and immediately use their new skills and strategies.

Integrated grammar instruction stems from the writing and reading activities, and gives students the know-how to write and edit their work with accuracy.

Tapestry Threads provide students with interesting facts and quotes that jumpstart classroom discussions.

Stimulating reading selections model writing and grammar usage, and prepare students for the pre-writing, writing, and revising activities.

Language Learning Strategies help students maximize their learning and become proficient in English.

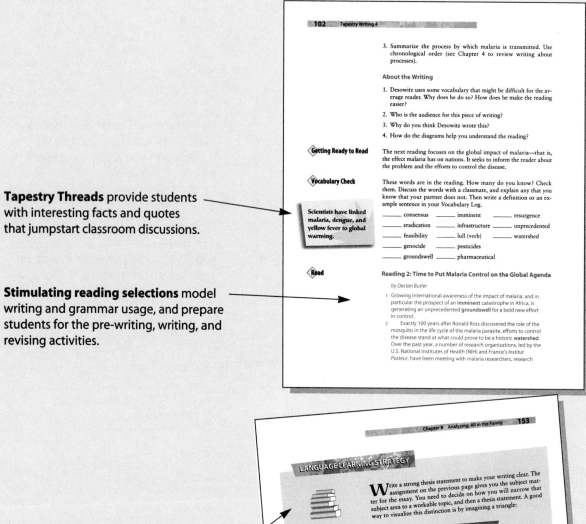

3. Summarize the process by which malaria is transmitted. Use chronological order (see Chapter 4 to review writing about processes).

About the Writing

1. Desowitz uses some vocabulary that might be difficult for the average reader. Why does he do so? How does he make the reading easier?

2. Who is the audience for this piece of writing?

3. Why do you think Desowitz wrote this?

4. How do the diagrams help you understand the reading?

Getting Ready to Read

The next reading focuses on the global impact of malaria—that is, the effect malaria has on nations. It seeks to inform the reader about the problem and the efforts to control the disease.

Vocabulary Check

These words are in the reading. How many do you know? Check them. Discuss the words with a classmate, and explain any that you know that your partner does not. Then write a definition or an example sentence in your Vocabulary Log.

Scientists have linked malaria, dengue, and yellow fever to global warming.

_____ consensus	_____ imminent	_____ resurgence
_____ eradication	_____ infrastructure	_____ unprecedented
_____ feasibility	_____ lull (verb)	_____ watershed
_____ genocide	_____ pesticides	
_____ groundswell	_____ pharmaceutical	

Read

Reading 2: Time to Put Malaria Control on the Global Agenda

by Declan Butler

1 Growing international awareness of the impact of malaria, and in particular the prospect of an **imminent** catastrophe in Africa, is generating an **unprecedented** **groundswell** for a bold new effort in control.

2 Exactly 100 years after Ronald Ross discovered the role of the mosquito in the life cycle of the malaria parasite, efforts to control the disease stand at what could prove to be a historic **watershed**. Over the past year, a number of research organizations, led by the U.S. National Institutes of Health (NIH) and France's *Institut Pasteur*, have been meeting with malaria researchers, research

LANGUAGE LEARNING STRATEGY

Write a strong thesis statement to make your writing clear. The assignment on the previous page gives you the subject matter for the essay. You need to decide on how you will narrow that subject area to a workable topic, and then a thesis statement. A good way to visualize this distinction is by imagining a triangle:

Subject: this is the broadest part of the triangle—"traditions in family life" in this assignment.

Topic: this narrows the subject further—for example, the importance of cultural traditions in immigrant families.

Thesis: this is the "point" of the triangle and of your paper. It presents an "argument." For example, a possible thesis might be: "Even though it is frustrating, it is important for immigrant parents to pass their cultural traditions on to their children."

For most types of college or expository writing, the success of your essay depends on a strong thesis statement. A thesis presents a specific argument or point you want to make.

Thesis statements are composed of two major elements: a topic and a comment. The topic is the part of the thesis that states generally what subject matter is discussed, and the comment specifies one important point relating to the topic. For example:

In the stories "Crickets" and "Grandma's Wake,"
└──────────────────────────┘
              topic

the theme of xxx plays an important role.
└──────────────────────────┘
              comment

(continued on next page)

Test-Taking Tips offer students practical steps for improving their test results.

Check Your Progress helps students monitor their own progress.

Test-Taking Tip

Read essay questions carefully before beginning an essay test. As you think of ideas and examples you will want to include in your essay, jot these down on a piece of scrap paper or on the back of the test so that you can remember what you want to include in your essay. This will also help you to keep your mind clear of details and to focus on the larger ideas you want to communicate in your essay.

CHECK YOUR PROGRESS

On a scale of 1 to 5, rate how well you have mastered the goals set at the beginning of the chapter:

1 2 3 4 5   reflect on what you already know about a topic.

1 2 3 4 5   discover resources on campus and in your community to help you with research.

1 2 3 4 5   get and give feedback on writing.

1 2 3 4 5   avoid sentence fragments.

1 2 3 4 5   (your own goal) _____

1 2 3 4 5   (your own goal) _____

If you've given yourself a 3 or lower on any of these goals:

- visit the *Tapestry* web site for additional practice.
- ask your instructor for extra help.
- review the sections of the chapter that you found difficult.
- work with a partner or study group to further your progress.

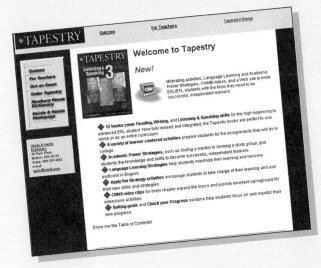

Expand your classroom at Tapestry Online
www.tapestry.heinle.com
- Online Quizzes
- Instructor's Manuals
- Opportunities to use and expand the Academic Power Strategies
- More!

◈ For a well-integrated curriculum, try the **Tapestry Reading** series and the **Tapestry Listening & Speaking** series, also from Heinle & Heinle.

◈ To learn more about the **Tapestry** principles, read *The Tapestry of Language Learning,* Second Edition, by Rebecca L. Oxford and Robin C. Scarcella, also from Heinle & Heinle Publishers. ISBN 0-8384-0994-6.

Memories are crucial to the act of writing.

—paraphrased from Georgia Heard

Read the quotation. According to Heard, what is important in writing? Which of your memories do you want to write about? Write your answers here:

_____

_____

_____

_____

I'LL NEVER FORGET . . .

Writing about yourself and your experiences is a common starting point for writers. Some begin by writing about their everyday activities, their feelings, and their hopes and dreams. Other writers begin with their past and with the people and events they can't forget. In this chapter, you're going to write about an unforgettable memory.

Setting Goals

In this chapter, you will practice narrating an event. Specifically, you will write about an unforgettable event from your past. In order to do this, you will:

◈ find a place where you do your best work.

◈ use past tense verbs correctly.

◈ use graphic organizers to generate and organize ideas.

◈ learn to use a thesaurus to expand your word choice.

What additional goals do you have for this chapter? Write them here:

_____

_____

_____

**Getting Started**   With a partner, talk about some unforgettable events from your past. What happened? Why do you remember these events?

MEETING THE TOPIC

Look at the photos of unforgettable events from the pasts of several student writers. Describe what you think is happening.

A.

B.

C.

D.

E.

A. _____

_____

B. _____

_____

C. _____

_____

D. _____

_____

E. _____

_____

> **Eleanor Roosevelt had an exceptionally good memory. She said her memory was good because she ate three cloves of garlic every day.**

Give and get information about the photos. Work with a classmate to describe the events in these photos. You may be able to describe one photo several ways. Use the following chart and add more descriptions if you can.

DESCRIPTION	PHOTO A	PHOTO B	PHOTO C	PHOTO D	PHOTO E
scary	_____	✔	_____	_____	_____
funny	_____	_____	_____	_____	_____
happy	_____	_____	_____	_____	_____
first time	_____	✔	_____	_____	_____
an event from childhood	_____	✔	_____	_____	_____
an unusual incident	_____	_____	_____	_____	_____
a common incident	_____	✔	_____	_____	_____
_____	_____	_____	_____	_____	_____
_____	_____	_____	_____	_____	_____

◆ **Freewrite**

You've had a chance to look, listen, and talk. Now put your ideas in writing. Write about one event from your past. Include everything you remember about the incident. Write notes or sentences, or make a list. Write as quickly as you can. Don't worry about grammar or spelling; just get your ideas on paper. You will expand this writing as you move through the activities in this chapter.

TUNING IN: "Hollywood Manicurist"

Beatrice Kaye is retired now, but fifty years ago she polished the nails of movie stars for MGM Studios in Hollywood. In the video, she describes this unforgettable period of her life. Read the questions and keep them in mind when you watch the video. Then go back and answer the questions. You may want to watch the video several times.

© CNN

The authors of *Live and Be Well* **recommend writing about your past experiences to improve your memory.**

1. What was Beatrice Kaye's job?

   a. She was a movie star costume designer.

   b. She was a movie star hairdresser.

   c. She was a barbershop manicurist.

2. What does the report say that Beatrice did?

   a. "Shop and shape."

   b. "Shape, shine, and keep a secret."

   c. "Shine and sell."

3. Which movie star is **not** mentioned in the video?

   a. Clark Gable

   b. Lana Turner

   c. Katherine Hepburn

   d. Nicole Kidman

   e. Madonna

   f. Spencer Tracy

4. Beatrice says she learned a lot about people by looking at their hands. What did she **not** say she learned about?

   a. jobs

   b. marriages

   c. children

5. Why will Beatrice never forget this period of her life?

   a. She earned lots of money.

   b. She worked with movie stars she admired.

   c. She decided to study acting.

ACADEMIC POWER STRATEGY

Find the place where you do your best work. If you know where you do your best work, you can save time and learn more effectively. Some students study best in quiet places like libraries or their rooms. Other students find it easier to concentrate in noisy places like coffee shops or student lounges. Think about the place where you do your best work.

Apply the Strategy

What do you need in order to study well? First check whether the features in Column 1 are important or unimportant. Then circle your preference in Column 2. Mark the descriptions that are right for you. Add information if you like. Discuss your answers with a partner.

WHERE DO YOU DO YOUR BEST WORK?

	COLUMN 1		COLUMN 2
	IMPORTANT	NOT IMPORTANT	THE SPACE SHOULD BE/HAVE:
1. Noise Level	_____	_____	loud quiet
2. Table Space	_____	_____	big tables individual desks
3. View	_____	_____	lots of windows no windows
4. Access to Resources	_____	_____	books, computers both neither
5. Location	_____	_____	near my home far from my home
6. Food/Drink	_____	_____	food, drink both neither
7. Other: _____	_____	_____	

I do my best work in this place: _____

_____

_____

EXPANDING YOUR LANGUAGE

··

◇**Vocabulary Check**

In each chapter of this book you will learn vocabulary to help you complete each writing assignment. Keep a separate notebook for vocabulary and expressions you want to remember and review regularly. This is your Vocabulary Log. Study these words and expressions people use when writing about memories. These terms come from the readings in this chapter. You will find them useful when you get ready to write. Check the words you already know. Find definitions for words that are new. Add new words to your Vocabulary Log.

———— autobiography   ———— to magnify

———— event   ———— to recall

———— incident   ———— to remember

———— memoir   ———— unforgettable

———— memorable   ———— used to be

———— past

◇**Vocabulary Tip**

Synonyms

Synonyms are different words that have the same (or a similar) meaning. Using synonyms helps you vary the words in your writing to make it more interesting. The following words are useful when writing about memories. Match the words on the left with their synonyms on the right.

common	remember
collect	unforgettable
imagine	enlarge
favorite	pretend
memorable	reveal
recall	best-loved
magnify	usual
incident	event
show	gather

◈ Vocabulary Building

Answer the following questions by writing about your experiences.

1. Many children play **imaginary** games. What did you **pretend** to do or be when you were young?

   _____

   _____

   _____

2. What was your **favorite** food when you were a child?

   _____

   _____

   _____

3. Think about an **event** from your past when you learned something very important. What did the lesson from this incident **reveal** about life or the world?

   _____

   _____

   _____

4. A **common** way to **remember** past events is to review old photos. Describe a **memorable** photo from your past.

   _____

   _____

   _____

5. Describe your **best-loved** teacher.

   _____

   _____

   _____

Grammar You Can Use: Past and Past Habitual Verb Tenses

When writing about events that have already occurred, the verbs are usually in the simple past tense *(play → played)* or past habitual *(play → used to play)*. Use the simple past tense for a completed action or actions:

I **played** on a soccer team in 1998.

Use the past habitual for a past action that occurred over a long time:

I **used to play** volleyball after school every day.

For regular verbs, form the past tense by adding *-ed (play → played)*, adding *-d (receive → received)*, or changing the *y* to *i* and adding *-ed (study → studied)*.

For irregular verbs, memorize the past tense forms. Begin by reviewing the common irregular verbs in the following list. Put an asterisk (*) by the verbs you still need to memorize.

COMMON IRREGULAR PAST TENSE VERB FORMS	
be/was	run/ran
become/became	say/said
fall/fell	see/saw
feel/felt	speak/spoke
get/got	stand/stood
go/went	take/took
have/had	tell/told
hear/heard	think/thought
know/knew	understand/understood
read/read	write/wrote

Complete the following paragraph by writing the simple past tense of the regular and irregular verbs.

The First Time I Went to School

Hunger of Memory **by Richard Rodriguez is the story of a Mexican American boy who begins school in Sacramento, California, knowing fifty words in English. He writes about his childhood memories as a non-native speaker.**

When I (to be) _____ eight years old, I (to go) _____ to school for the first time. One month before school began, my parents (to become) _____ very busy and (to take) _____ a lot of interest in me. My father (to study) _____ information from several schools. My mother (to tell) _____ all of my cousins' families to help me prepare for school. One week before school began, I (to receive) _____ a lot of presents. I (to get) _____ a new school bag, a couple of new books, and some pencils. I (to feel) _____ like the owner of a school supply store. The night before school began, I (to be) _____ so excited that I could not fall asleep. I woke up late. Luckily, my mother (to be) _____ ready. She (to help) _____ me get dressed in my new clothes. I (to pack) _____ all my new school equipment. On that happy day I (to start) _____ my life as a student.

—Kevin Lam

READING FOR WRITING

One of the best ways to improve your writing is to read other people's work. Read these descriptions of unforgettable events. The first reading selection is about a time the writer was very naughty. The second selection is a memory about the writer's father and his scrolls. (Scrolls are sheets of paper painted with designs. They are kept rolled up or hung on walls.) As you read, look for language and ideas that you can use when you write about your own unforgettable event.

◆ **Getting Ready to Read**   Before you read, answer these questions:

- What does *naughty* mean?
- Does *naughty* usually describe children or adults?
- What is an example of a child's *naughty* action?
- Were you ever naughty as a child?

◆ **Read**   **Reading 1: A Naughty Child**

I used to be a very naughty girl in my childhood. That is hard for my friends to imagine now. One time I played with matches, and I nearly burned the living room. Another time I cut paper on my bed and cut the sheets too. I caused lots of trouble. I was a terrible child. One of the most horrible things that I did was at a wedding. Everyone was enjoying the food and beverages. There was one man there, drinking a little wine, and he stood up to make a toast to the bride and groom. "Congratulations," he said in a loud, deep voice. "I am proud to be here today to celebrate this occasion." Everyone listened to his speech. While he was talking, I moved his chair away. No one noticed. When he finished his speech, he went to sit down and fell on the ground. People jumped up to help him. They laughed. "You must be drunk!" they said. Nobody knew the truth. That is the naughtiest thing I ever did. You will be happy to know that I am very different now.

—Anne Chen-Han Li

◆ **After You Read**   1. What is something naughty the writer did as a child?

_____

2. Where was the writer when she was most naughty?

_____

3. What did she do at the wedding?

_____

_____

4. How does she feel now about this naughty incident? How do you know?

_____

_____

5. Were you ever naughty as a child? If so, what did you do?

_____

_____

Getting Ready to Read

Before you read, answer these questions:

- Do you remember something one of your relatives always did?

- Does anyone in your family have special objects from his or her past?

Read

Reading 2: My Father's Scrolls

I **remember** how on certain Sunday evenings my father would show us his best-loved possessions, unrolling across our dining-room table the hundred-year-old scrolls he carried over the sea from China. He showed them to us in the order he remembered having collected them, and the first one, unscrolled,[1] revealed first the black claws, and then the long legs, and at last the whole height of a standing crane,[2] long-beaked, with coarse head and neck feathers, and one fierce eye. The second scroll was mostly white except for the blight-struck[3] pine, and one bird perched at the tip: a shrike,[4] surviving, a carrier of seed and stones in his little gizzard.[5] The scrolls in my father's house, stored in room after room, or hung in the halls, were so many any breeze could send their silk dancing and their bones all knocking against the walls.

—Li-Young Lee

[1]**unscrolled:** unrolled, opened
[2]**crane:** a kind of bird
[3]**blight-struck:** diseased
[4]**shrike:** a kind of bird
[5]**gizzard:** the second stomach of a bird

◆ **After You Read**

1. How old are the scrolls?

   _____

2. Where are they from?

   _____

   _____

3. How does the writer's father feel about the scrolls? How do you know?

   _____

   _____

4. Why do you think the writer chose to write about his father's scrolls?

   _____

   _____

FROM READING TO WRITING

◆ **Getting Ready to Write**   Answer the following questions to prepare for the writing assignment in this chapter. These exercises use the reading selections to teach you about writing.

1. Why did the writers write about the specific memories they chose? What was the significance or meaning of those memories for each of the writers? Review the selections, talk with a classmate, and write down what was important about the memories for each writer. After you have filled in the chart for the other writers, think about an important memory for yourself. What is its meaning for you? You may choose to write about this memory for this chapter's assignment.

Writer	Memory	What Was Important About the Memory
Anne Chen-Han Li	being naughty as a child	
Li-Young Lee	his father's scrolls	
You		

2. Study how the writers in the two selections give specific details about the people they admire. Go back to the reading selections and <u>underline</u> words, phrases, or sentences that include specific details.

3. Look for conversation in "A Naughty Child" and highlight it. Did it help you imagine the people in the event more clearly?

> One way to improve your memory is to take pills from the ginkgo biloba tree. Originally from Asia, the tree is resistant to time, weather, and disease.

Writing About a Memory

When you describe an event from the past, there are a few things you can do to expand your writing and make it interesting to read. These tips will help the reader imagine your experiences and feelings. First, choose an event that you have a lot to write about. Second, make the event "come alive" to the reader by "magnifying" it, or expanding each thought or action. Finally, include dialogue so that the event is more immediate and alive for the reader. You can practice these tips in the following exercises.

Choose an Unforgettable Event You Remember Well

The first step in writing is to choose a topic. Writers do best when they choose a topic they can write a lot about. Many writers begin by thinking of lots of possibilities.

LANGUAGE LEARNING STRATEGY

Use graphic organizers to help you generate and organize ideas. A **mindmap,** a type of graphic organizer, is a "picture" of ideas. Mindmapping can help you choose a topic for your writing. There are many kinds of mindmaps. You can use a mindmap to understand ideas in something you have read or when you are preparing to write.

One kind of mindmap is a **cluster.** A cluster is a group of idea categories. You can use it to help you remember different events from your past. The next page shows an example of a cluster a student started before writing about an unforgettable memory:

(continued on next page)

Unforgettable Events from My Past

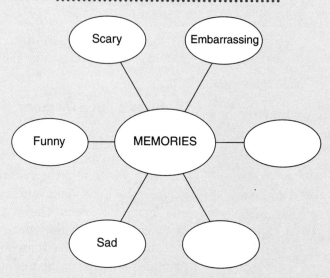

Can you think of any other categories?

Now, take a look at this student's next step:

Funny Events

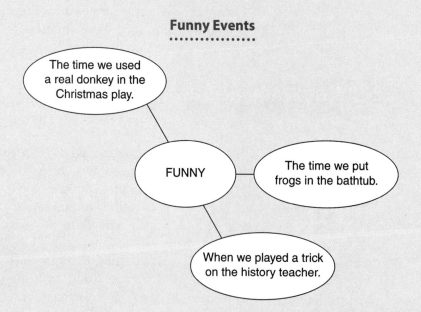

In this cluster, the student took one of the categories and gave examples for it.

Apply the Strategy

Make your own cluster of unforgettable events. Start with "Memories" (Step 1), as the student did in the example. Then, for Step 2, take one of your categories and give at least three examples.

Step 1:

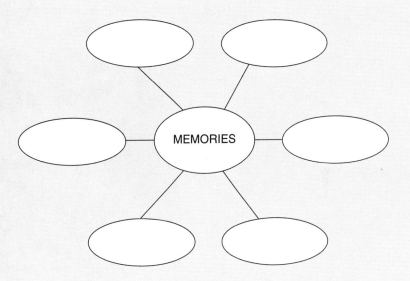

Step 2:

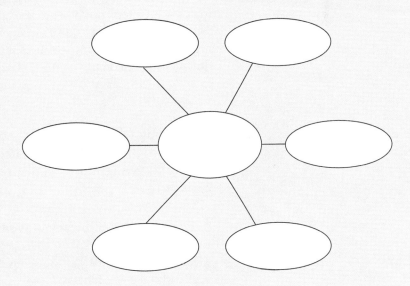

Expand Your Writing by Including Details

When you write about a past event, you want the reader to imagine the specific actions, sights, sounds, and feelings that you experienced. One way to do this is to magnify the incident by expanding what happened. You can do this by adding sentences to each part of the event to show or explain more specifically what happened. Read how one writer took one event and expanded it.

Bicycle Adventure (A)
. . . .

(1) When I was a little girl, I rode my bicycle every afternoon. (2) One day I met my sister, and we decided to ride to a new place. (3) We took our bikes to the hill in our neighborhood. (4) When we began to ride, I discovered that the brakes on my bike didn't work. (5) I crashed at the bottom of the hill. (6) My sister fell on top of me. (7) I will never forget that day.

—Luz Zamora

The paragraph tells about a childhood memory, but it is difficult to imagine the sights, sounds, or feelings of the event. By taking each sentence and giving more details, the writer makes the adventure come alive:

Bicycle Adventure (B)
. . . .

(1) When I was a little girl, I rode my bicycle every afternoon.
My bike was blue and shiny.
I loved to ride it around my neighborhood after school.
I spent an hour on it before going home every night.

(2) One day I met my sister, and we decided to ride to a new place.

My sister was much more daring than I was.

She was also stronger and more confident.

(3) We took our bikes to the hill in our neighborhood.

My sister said she wanted to ride fast.

I didn't think the hill was steep, so I agreed.

I was excited to be going somewhere new.

(4) When we began to ride, I discovered that the brakes on my bike didn't work.

I squeezed and squeezed the brakes, but the bike went faster, not slower.

How did I know my brakes didn't work?

I started to panic.

My sister was laughing and shouting.

She pretended she was riding a horse.

(5) I crashed at the bottom of the hill.

My bike hit a rock, and the front wheel turned.

I fell to the ground.

My leg got caught in the bike.

(6) My sister fell on top of me.

She was right behind me yelling at her horse.

My sister, her bike-horse, my bike, and I were in a pile at the bottom of the hill.

(7) I will never forget that day.

I broke my leg, and my sister hurt her arm.

When I got home from the hospital, my sister drew on my cast.

She drew a horse that said "Sorry!"

Now read the new paragraph:

Bicycle Adventure (C)

When I was a little girl, I rode my bicycle every afternoon. My bike was blue and shiny. I loved to ride it around my neighborhood after school. I spent an hour on it before going home every night. One day I met my sister, and we decided to ride to a new place. My sister was much more daring than I was. She was also stronger and more confident. We took our bikes to the hill in our neighborhood. My sister said she wanted to ride fast. I didn't think the hill was steep, so I agreed. I was excited to be going somewhere new. When we began to ride, I discovered that the brakes on my bike didn't work. I squeezed and squeezed on the brakes, but the bike went faster, not slower. How did I know my brakes didn't work? I started to panic. My sister was laughing and shouting. She pretended she was riding a horse. I crashed at the bottom of the hill. My bike hit a rock, and the front wheel turned. I fell to the ground. My leg got caught in the bike. My sister fell on top of me. She was right behind me yelling at her horse. My sister, her bike-horse, my bike, and I were in a pile at the bottom of the hill. I will never forget that day. I broke my leg, and my sister hurt her arm. When I got home from the hospital, my sister drew on my cast. She drew a horse that said "Sorry!"

Practice

1. The writer added different kinds of details in Paragraph B. Each detail answers a question. Go back to Paragraph B and match the questions to the details.

   a. What did you do?

   b. What did you see?

   c. How did you feel?

   d. What did you hear?

   e. Why do you remember?

2. Start with Paragraph A. Add your own details. Share your new paragraph with your class.

3. Practice adding details to this paragraph. Add different kinds of details; then share what you wrote with a classmate.

Mountain View
· · · · · · · · · · · · · · · · ·

(1) I **remember** the first time I went to the mountain. (2) I was with my brother and his friends. (3) We climbed the mountain and looked down. (4) We saw small, green rice fields, vegetable fields, and a few ponds. (5) We also saw lots of people working in the fields. (6) It looked like many colorful butterflies dancing on a green stage. (7) I was so excited that I forgot how tired I was.

—Tharavouth Tan

(1) I remember the first time I went to the mountain.

_____

_____

_____

(2) I was with my brother and his friends.

_____

_____

_____

(3) We climbed the mountain and looked down.

_____

_____

_____

(4) We saw small, green rice fields, vegetable fields, and a few ponds.

_____

_____

_____

(5) We also saw lots of people working in the fields.

_____

_____

_____

(6) It looked like many colorful butterflies dancing on a green stage.

_____

_____

_____

(7) I was so excited that I forgot how tired I was.

_____

_____

_____

4. Now write your own paragraph. First write a few sentences that tell about the incident. This is a "skeleton." Then add details for each sentence.

(1) _____

_____

_____

(2) _____

_____

_____

_____

(3) _____

_____

_____

_____

(4) _____

_____

_____

_____

(5) _____

_____

_____

_____

(6) _____

_____

_____

_____

(7) _____

_____

_____

_____

Include Dialogue

Another way to make your writing lively and interesting is to include dialogue, or conversation. This makes the event more immediate for the reader. When you want to include conversation in your writing, follow these guidelines:

- Enclose anything someone says directly in quotation marks:

  "Congratulations," he said in a loud, deep voice.

- When the speaker changes, move to the next line:

  "I am proud to be here today to celebrate this occasion," he said before he fell down.

  "You must be drunk!" they said.

Read how dialogue makes these events more immediate, as if the reader is there too.

- Example 1: One day I met my sister, and we decided to ride to a new place. My sister was much more daring than I was. She was also stronger and more confident. "Let's ride down the hill," my sister said. "I want to go really fast!"

- Example 2: My sister was laughing and shouting. She pretended she was riding a horse. "Giddyup, giddyup, you slow horse. Yahoooooooooo!"

Practice Add dialogue to make these details more lively and immediate:

I remember the first time I went to the mountain. I was with my brother and his friends.

_____

_____

_____

_____

_____

We also saw lots of people working in the fields. It looked like many colorful butterflies dancing on a green stage.

_____

_____

_____

_____

Choose a Topic

Now decide the specific topic of your writing for this chapter. You may use the topic you wrote about on page 5 or choose from the following list. Write about an unforgettable memory because it was:

- scary
- the first time you did something
- very happy
- very sad
- very funny
- a combination of these

LANGUAGE LEARNING STRATEGY

Learn to use a thesaurus to expand your word choice. A **thesaurus** is a dictionary of synonyms and a useful tool for writers. Refer to a thesaurus when you want to vary the words in your writing. By using a thesaurus, you can avoid overusing certain words. Ask your classmates or teacher where you can find a thesaurus to use or buy.

Apply the Strategy

Review the list of synonyms you studied on page 8. Use a thesaurus to find several synonyms for the following words, which you may overuse in writing about memories.

unforgettable: _____

memory: _____

happy: _____

past: _____

Study a Student Example

Read this paragraph that a college student wrote. Write answers to the questions following the reading; then share your answers in class.

A Weekend at Grandmother's

One weekend some cousins and I went to our grandmother's house. She had a beautiful house outside Mexico City. On Sunday we organized a game with balloons filled with water. It was warm and sunny. The game was between girls and boys. It was so much fun that some of our uncles began to play too. Some hours later, about one o'clock, my grandmother called us to come eat lunch. Nobody paid attention to her. We all continued playing. About twenty minutes later, she came out again and said: "I'm very, very angry now because nobody listened to me the first time." At that moment one water balloon fell on her head, and she was completely wet. She started to laugh so happily that I can't forget this moment.

—Margarita Esponda

1. Why did the grandmother get angry?

   a. She doesn't like sunny weather.

   b. No one came to eat lunch when she called.

   c. She doesn't like balloons.

2. Why did everyone at the party start laughing?

   _____

   _____

   _____

> When you want to learn something you'll need to remember soon (short-term memory), study in the morning. Long-term memory powers are strongest in the afternoon.

3. What did you notice or like about this student example?

_____

_____

_____

4. What question or suggestion do you have for this writer?

_____

_____

_____

Write

Now you're ready to write. Write about an unforgettable event from your past. Choose a memory that is important to you and one you can write a lot about. Expand the event to include specific details that show what happened. Include dialogue if it helps the reader hear and imagine the people from the incident. You may use the writing you've already begun in this chapter. Do your writing in a place where you do your best work.

After You Write

Revise

After writing a draft of your essay, it is useful to have someone else read it so that you know how you can add or take away parts to improve it. In this stage of the writing process, you are looking at ideas. Exchange your paper with a classmate, or give your paper to your teacher or another reader to evaluate by answering these questions:

Questions for Editing	Yes	No
1. Has the writer described an event from the past? Notes:		
2. Has the writer explained what happened, when it happened, and who was there? Notes:		

Questions for Revision	Yes	No
3. Has the writer expanded the event by including specific details so that the reader can imagine the actions sights, sounds, and feelings? Notes:		
4. Has the writer explained why this event is unforgettable? Notes:		
5. Would you like to know something else about the event? If yes, write down something the writer should add:		

Plan your revision by reading the checklist. Talk with your teacher or classmates about what you can do to improve this assignment. Write some notes in case you choose to rewrite this paper.

Edit

After revising your essay, you should review it for spelling, punctuation, and grammar. In this stage of the writing process, you are looking for correctness. Read and respond to this checklist alone; then exchange your paper with a classmate and answer these questions:

Questions for Editing	Yes	No
1. Is there a title that tells the reader the topic of the writing? Notes:		
2. Does the writer use past tense verbs correctly? Notes:		
3. Does the writer use vocabulary from this chapter correctly? Notes:		

Questions for Editing	Yes	No
4. Is dialogue enclosed in quotation marks? Notes:		
5. Are there any grammar mistakes you want to point out? If yes, write what the writer should check:		

Keep all of the writing you do for this class in a folder called a Writing Portfolio. You will look through this folder to review your progress and choose papers to rewrite. Correct any mistakes your classmate or teacher pointed out in the Editing Checklist. Now you are ready to place your writing in your Writing Portfolio. You may want to rewrite it now or expand it to a longer piece later.

PUTTING IT ALL TOGETHER

Use What You Have Learned

Write about another event from the past. Use what you learned in this chapter to make your paragraph interesting and correct. Refer to your teacher's or classmate's comments on your first paragraph. When you are finished, put your writing in your Writing Portfolio.

Test-Taking Tip

Find out everything you can about a test before the day of the test. Ask your instructor questions like: When and where is the test? What chapters or topics will be covered? What types of questions will be asked? Will it be an open- or closed-book test? What should I bring to the test? How will the test be graded?

Knowing what to expect will help you feel more prepared and confident on the day of the test.

CHECK YOUR PROGRESS

On a scale of 1 to 5, where 1 means "not at all," 2 means "not very well," 3 means "moderately well," 4 means "well," and 5 means "very well," rate how well you have mastered the goals set at the beginning of the chapter:

1 2 3 4 5   write about an unforgettable event from your past.

1 2 3 4 5   find a place where you do your best work.

1 2 3 4 5   use past tense verbs correctly.

1 2 3 4 5   use graphic organizers to generate and organize ideas.

1 2 3 4 5   use a thesaurus to expand your word choice.

If you've given yourself a 3 or lower on any of these goals:

- visit the *Tapestry* web site for additional practice.
- ask your instructor for extra help.
- review the sections of the chapter that you found difficult.
- work with a partner or study group to further your progress.

"Everyone has at least one hero—someone who moves us beyond ourselves and gives us hope for the future."

—Anonymous

According to the quotation, what do heroes do for us? Do you agree that everyone has a hero? Write down a few of your own ideas about why people are heroes:

_____

_____

_____

_____

PERSONAL HEROES

Our families, our friends, and our teachers are strong influences in our lives. These people show us how to do things and teach us what to believe. They also help us make important decisions. In this chapter, you will think about the important people in your life and write about someone you admire.

Setting Goals

In this chapter, you will practice describing a person. Specifically, you will write about a person you admire. You will describe this person and tell about an event. You will explain how this person has influenced you. In order to do this, you will:

- find a mentor to help you in and out of school.
- practice learning vocabulary in "chunks" so that you can use new words correctly right away.
- learn when and how to use the past perfect tense.
- learn specific language for an assignment to make your writing precise.

What additional goals do you have for this chapter? Write them here:

_____

_____

◆**Getting Started**

Write down the names of some people you admire. Are they famous? Are they friends or family? What do you admire about them? Share your ideas with a classmate.

_____

_____

_____

MEETING THE TOPIC

Look at the photos of six people who have been important in the lives of others. The photos show some special qualities each of these people has. Jot down words, phrases, or expressions that describe the people in the photos.

A.

B.

C.

D.

E.

F.

> . . . like most boys,
> I thought my dad
> could do anything.
> He could drive, paint,
> name the constellations,
> set up a tent and had
> been in the air force—
> what else was there?
>
> **— MARK SALZMAN**

A. _____

_____

B. _____

_____

C. _____

_____

D. _____

_____

E. _____

_____

F. _____

_____

Give and get information about the photos. Expand on your ideas in the following chart. You wrote words, phrases, and expressions to describe the people in the photos. Now write a sentence about them. Share what you write with at least three classmates. Collect some more descriptive words about the people in the photos from your classmates' ideas.

Photo	Descriptive Words, Phrases, and Sentences
A.	
B.	
C.	
D.	
E.	
F.	

Freewrite

After looking at photos and talking with your classmates about personal heroes, here's your first chance to put your ideas in writing. Write about a person you admire. You can write about someone you know now or someone from your past. Write for ten minutes without stopping. Don't worry about grammar or spelling; just get your ideas on paper. You will use these ideas for the writing assignment later in the chapter.

TUNING IN: "Coach, Teacher, Friend"

© CNN

Coach, Teacher, Friend

Think about someone in your community whom everyone admires. The CNN video you will watch is about someone like this—a person many people admire. He has been at his current job for five decades. How old do you think he is? Read the questions, watch the video, and then answer the questions.

1. What does Ralph Tasker do?

    a. He's a retired college professor.

    b. He's a high school basketball coach.

    c. He's a college basketball coach.

2. How has Coach Tasker made a difference in the lives of his players?

    a. Some have won college scholarships.

    b. Some have become professional basketball players.

    c. Both of these.

3. What are three ways people have described Tasker?

    a. _____

    b. _____

    c. _____

4. Which of these does Coach Tasker **not** believe?

    a. "The game mirrors life."

    b. "Individual skills come first."

    c. "The team comes first."

5. If you were going to write about Coach Tasker, which of the following qualities would you choose to emphasize? Why?

   a. He never gives up.

   b. He believes that you have to "get up when you're knocked down."

   c. He believes that the team comes first.

   _____

ACADEMIC POWER STRATEGY

Find a mentor to help you in and out of school. A mentor is someone who can help you and give you advice. This person can help explain homework assignments for your classes, read and respond to your writing, or answer a question about English. A mentor can also help you outside of school. This person can give you advice about places to visit, how to spend holidays, or how to travel on public transportation. A mentor can make your life easier.

Apply the Strategy

Think of a person who can be your mentor. Perhaps you can find more than one mentor. Write the name of a person (or people) you know to complete each of these sentences:

1. _____ is someone I talk to regularly.

2. _____ knows about English and can help me with the language.

3. _____ knows about school and can help me choose courses and buy books and supplies.

4. _____ can help me get to know the area where I live, work, or study, and can tell me about places I should visit.

Think of some other ways a mentor can help you. Add them to your list.

5. _____

6. _____

Use your mentor. This person is a valuable learning resource.

EXPANDING YOUR LANGUAGE

Learn new words in chunks to use them correctly right away. While it is useful to learn new vocabulary words to improve your writing (as you did in Chapter 1), it is still more efficient to learn vocabulary in chunks, or groups of words that show how the word is used. By learning vocabulary in chunks, you can use new words correctly right away.

Apply the Strategy

All of the vocabulary words for this chapter are presented below in chunks. Study these expressions. They are from the reading selections you will read later in this chapter. Check the expressions you already know and find meanings for those that are new. Add them to your Vocabulary Log.

_____ as I remember it,

_____ certain moments resonate

_____ from the start

_____ strong in body and spirit

_____ to be grateful for something

_____ to be old enough to do something

_____ to be passionate about something

_____ to find one's way

_____ to have a hard time

_____ to have an influence on someone

_____ to imagine oneself somewhere or doing something

_____ to leave indelible imprints on my life

_____ to like the way someone does something

_____ to look up to someone

◇Vocabulary Tip

Compound Adjectives

You can use words you already know to form new words. By combining nouns and verbs, you can make adjectives that are specific and descriptive. Look at these examples. You will read them again in the reading selections.

> *We entered the* **candle-lit** *church.*

> *It was a little red leather book with* **gilt-edged** *pages.*

These compound adjectives join a **noun** (person, place, or thing) or **adjective** (a word that describes a noun) and **the past participle of the verb** (*light → lit*) with a **hyphen** (-). Write sentences that explain the meaning of each of the compound adjectives below:

1. We entered the **candle-lit** church.

   EXAMPLE: *The candles provided light in the church.*

   _____

   _____

   _____

   _____

2. It was a little red leather book with **gilt-edged** pages.

   _____

   _____

   _____

   _____

3. She bought some **peach-colored** flowers.

   _____

   _____

   _____

   _____

4. The woman wore **funny-shaped** pants to ride horses.

   _____

   _____

   _____

   _____

◇Vocabulary Building

1. Match the following expressions in Column 1 to expressions with the same meaning in Column 2.

to look up to someone	to really love something
to have an influence on someone	since the beginning
to be passionate about something	to find something difficult
to leave indelible imprints on my life	to admire someone
from the start	to affect someone
to have a hard time	to create unforgettable memories

2. Use the vocabulary chunks below to complete the following paragraph.

from the start   liked the way my father taught

was old enough to   imagined himself

was passionate about   had a great influence on me

I am grateful for

(1) _____ my dad wanted me

to be mechanical. He (2) _____

repairing small machines. When he thought about the future,

he (3) _____ in the workshop

of his famous son, a successful mechanical genius. As soon

as I (4) _____ use my hands,

my father gave me a flashlight to assemble. I figured out

how to put all the pieces together. He gave me many small

mechanical problems to solve. My dad was a patient teacher.

I (5) _____. He (6) _____.

I can still figure out how to put pieces together. Now I repair

computers, and my dad visits me in my workshop often.

(7) _____ my father's early

teaching.

3. Answer the following questions by writing sentences about people you know or knew. Use the "chunks" from the Language Learning Strategy on page 36.

a. How old were you when you **were old enough to spend time** away from home without your parents?

_____

_____

_____

b. Write about **a moment that resonates** when you think of someone from your past that you admire.

_____

_____

_____

c. Which two people **have left an indelible imprint on your life?**

_____

_____

_____

d. When have you been somewhere and **imagined yourself somewhere else?** Where were you? What did you imagine was happening?

_____

_____

_____

e. Think about someone you admire. What do you **like about the way this person does something?**

_____

_____

_____

f. Describe a period in your life when you **had a hard time.**

_____

_____

_____

READING FOR WRITING

Reading before writing helps writers gather ideas and language. In this chapter, you will read selections by two writers who describe people they admire. Look for different ways each writer develops a description of her hero.

◇ Getting Ready to Read

Before you read, answer these questions:

- What's an accordion? Have you ever seen one? Have you ever played one?

- What do you know about Sweden, Swedish customs, or the Swedish language?

- What does it mean to be "strong in body and spirit"?

◇ Read

> **My father didn't tell me how to live; he lived, and let me watch him do it.**
>
> —CLARENCE
> BUDDINTON KELLARD

Reading 1: Aunt June

1   Life happens when we are young, and then, one day, we **are old enough to** reflect, to look back, and to see patterns, connections, and directions that we didn't see earlier. My earliest memories of my Aunt June are sketchy in details, yet, looking back, **certain moments resonate,** and these moments **have left indelible imprints on my life.**

2   I admired my Aunt June **from the start.** She was **strong in body and spirit.** She **was passionate about** life and learning. When I was nine years old, I decided I wanted to be like her. **I liked the way** she read books to her kids, a cup of cold coffee nearby. I liked the way she sang in Swedish and danced. She had so many stories to tell, so many pictures to show. June loved flowers. She taught me that the best way to keep them fresh is to make a diagonal slice across each stem. She was one of my first teachers outside the classroom.

3   At a Christmas smorgasborg[1] at my house a few years ago, Aunt June made the Swedish glogg.[2] She played the accordion while my Uncle Ken danced with his sister, my mother. After only a few hours of sleep that night, we arose in the dark, cold morning to attend the early Christmas Day service in Swedish at the Lutheran church in San Francisco. We **found our way** through the

[1]**smorgasborg:** many kinds of food spread on tables for people to serve themselves

[2]**Swedish glogg:** Christmas drink

fog to the candle-lit church. We tried to follow the Swedish words in the songs. June, the only one in our family able to speak Swedish, smiled, laughed, and sang. I **imagined myself** in Sweden . . . or perhaps in a Swedish film. Aunt June was the director.

4   The last time I sat with June on a Saturday morning in her bedroom, she **was having a hard time** breathing and getting comfortable. On a table in front of her was a bouquet of peach-colored tulips. There was also a bouquet of daisies, her favorite flowers. June's eyes opened and closed, lazily. She was uncomfortable in the bed, until suddenly she sat forward, opened her eyes wide and said, her voice as strong as in church that Christmas morning, "Oh, look at the flowers." And we did.

—Audrey Fielding

After You Read

1. Why did the writer admire her Aunt June? Give two reasons.

    a. _____

    b. _____

2. How old was the writer when she decided she wanted to be like her aunt? _____

3. What are three things the writer learned from her aunt?

    a. _____

    b. _____

    c. _____

4. What did Aunt June do at Christmas in San Francisco a few years ago? _____

_____

5. What does the last sentence ('And we did') mean? What did they do? _____

_____

Getting Ready to Read

The second selection is about the writer's mother. In this piece, the writer wonders about her mother before she got married and had children. She finds several objects that represent this early period of her mother's life. Before you read, answer these questions:

- What do you know about your parents' life before they got married?

- Are there objects from your mother's or father's past that you wonder about?

Read

Reading 2: Around the Corner

1 When I was small, maybe seven or eight, I noticed some crinkled leather boots in my mother's closet, some I knew I had never seen her wear. She told me they were for horseback riding, and showed me some funny-shaped pants. "They're jodhpurs," she said, and spelled it for me. She said she'd ridden when she was in college. She had taken archery, too. She had planned to major in journalism so she could meet with world leaders, and she had interviewed the university president for the student newspaper. She had taken Spanish, and sometimes spoke phrases of it around the house: "You're *loco en la cabeza,*"[1] she would say to my father, and she had taught me to count from *uno* to *diez.*[2] She also knew another language: shorthand. Her mother had made her take it because it was practical, and my mother had used it when she worked as a secretary at the truck line. She wrote her Christmas lists in shorthand—and anything else she didn't want me or my father to read, like her diary. It was a little red leather book with gilt-edged pages, and I was most intrigued by its little gold lock. **As I remember it,** my mother showed it to me, and maybe even read some passages to me. Looking over her shoulder I could see that some parts were in shorthand. When I asked what they said, she just laughed and turned the page.

[1]*loco en la cabeza:* crazy

[2]**from *uno* to *diez*:** from one to ten

2   My mother seemed to treat the diary—and the boots and jodhpurs, the glamorous picture of herself that she had sent to my father overseas, her dreams of becoming a famous journalist—as relics of a distant past that no longer had much to do with her. She had left them all behind for life with my father and me, and eventually my two brothers. I loved my mother and thought she was beautiful. I **was grateful for** the sort of mother she was—she had milk and cookies waiting when I came home from school, packed my lunchbox each morning. Every holiday was full of treats and surprises: a present by my plate on Valentine's Day, eggs hidden all over the house on Easter morning, Kool-Aid in my thermos on my birthday. Yet at the same time that I basked in the attention my mother lavished on me, I was haunted by the image of the person who seemed to have disappeared around the corner just before I arrived.

—Sharon Bryan

◆After You Read

1. What are two objects that represent the mother's life before she married and had children?

   a. _____

   b. _____

2. What did the mother write in shorthand? Why?

   _____

   _____

3. What is one thing the mother did that the writer was grateful for?

   _____

   _____

4. What do you think the writer means by her last sentence?

_____

_____

◇ **Grammar You Can Use: Past Perfect Tense**

In this chapter, you will write about people you know now and knew in your past. If writing about the past, you will want to use the correct verb tense. When writing about events that occurred *before* a time in the past, use the **past perfect tense** *(play → had played).*

I **played** on a soccer team in 1998. Before that, I **had played** volleyball.

before 1998	1998	now
volleyball	soccer	

Form the past perfect by putting *had* before the past participle of the verb.

1. Go back to "Around the Corner" and underline the verbs in the past perfect tense.

2. In Chapter 1, you read about some special family scrolls. In this chapter, you also read about some special family objects. Write at least three sentences about one or more special objects in your family. Use the past perfect tense at least once.

_____

_____

_____

_____

_____

FROM READING TO WRITING

Answer the following questions to prepare for the writing assignment in this chapter. These exercises use the reading selections to teach you about writing.

1. Why did the writers write about the specific people they chose? Why were they personal heroes? How did they influence the writers?

Review the selections, talk with a classmate, and write down what was important about these heroes for each writer. Fill in the chart. Then think about a person you admire. Why did you choose this person? Fill in the chart for your personal hero. You will develop these ideas for this chapter's assignment.

Writer	Person	What Was Important About the Person
Audrey Fielding	her aunt	
Sharon Bryan	her mother	
You		

2. What specific details did the writers in the two selections use to describe the people they admire? Go back to the reading selections and underline phrases or sentences that describe Aunt June and Bryan's mother.

3. What short stories do the writers tell to show something about the people they admire? Go back to the reading selections and highlight the incidents you read that show something important about Aunt June and Bryan's mother.

Getting Ready to Write

Writing About a Person You Admire

When you write about a personal hero, there are a few things you can do to help your reader "get to know" the person you're describing. Practice these tips for the writing assignment in this chapter.

LANGUAGE LEARNING STRATEGY

Learn specific language for the assignment to make your writing precise. Different writing assignments require special words and sentence types. For example, when writing about memories, you use different words than when you write about names. Learn specific

(continued on next page)

vocabulary that reflects the topic of your assignment. When writing about people you admire, review adjectives that describe people.

Use Descriptive Adjectives About People

Vivid adjectives are powerful tools when writing about people. You can divide these words into two groups: adjectives that describe someone's physical characteristics (what a person looks like), and adjectives that describe someone's personality (how a person acts). Read these groups of words and add few of your own adjectives to each group.

Physical Characteristics			Personality Characteristics		
tall	short	stocky	friendly	shy	open
strong	thin	attractive	reserved	happy	warm
heavy	skinny	fat	quiet	cheerful	_____
muscular	petite	good-looking			
_____	_____	_____	_____	_____	_____

Apply the Strategy

Share the words you added to each group. Then look at the following photos. First write physical descriptions of the people in the photos. Then write sentences about their personalities.

> **A hero is an ordinary person who performs an ordinary task in an extraordinary situation.**
>
> **—UNKNOWN**

Focus Your Description

When you write about someone you admire, think of one important quality to emphasize and illustrate. Perhaps your personal hero is generous or loyal or patient or kind. Emphasizing one quality will give your description a focus. Read the descriptions of these three people. Choose a quality you would like to emphasize if you were writing about them. Explain your choice.

Descriptions	What Would You Emphasize and Why?
Alp is an excellent cook has dinner parties often gives home-baked food as gifts takes cooking classes learned to cook from his Turkish mother	
Beth is passionate about her work trains teachers reads professional books in her free time believes that she is making a difference has lots of energy	
Frederique is a painter earns money by repairing boats lives in a small apartment doesn't earn much money studies classical artists doesn't care much about money is bilingual	

Tell a Story About the Person

In order to show the reader what the person is like, describe an event or tell a brief story to illustrate the quality you have chosen to emphasize. Review the "stories" the writers included in the two reading selections you read. Use these as models for your own writing.

Practice Tell a story about your personal hero. Choose an event that shows how this person has the quality you have chosen to emphasize. When you are finished, read your story to a classmate. Does your story show what you wanted to show?

Tell How the Person Has Influenced You

Make sure you show the reader how your personal hero has influenced you. Use the readings as models as you get ready to write about a person you admire. Go back to the reading selections and complete the following chart.

Title	What quality about the person does the writer emphasize?	What event(s) does the writer describe?	How has the person influenced the writer?
Aunt June			
Around the Corner			

Choose a Topic

Now decide the specific topic of your writing for this chapter. Choose a person who:

- taught you something important
- has the qualities you want to have
- helped you achieve something
- has influenced you to become who you are today

Plan Your Writing

Use this graphic organizer to plan your writing:

Introduction: Person You Are Writing About

Paragraph 1: Description of the Person

Paragraph 2: One Quality You Want to Emphasize

Paragraph 3: A Story That Shows This Quality

Conclusion: How the Person Has Influenced You

Study a Student Example

As you prepare to write, read the following essay that a college student wrote. Then answer the questions.

Vietnamese Punk Rocker

· ·

Oanh was in my computer class last semester, but she didn't look like a student at all. She often wore t-shirts to school that had words on them such as "Love Me" and "Kiss Me," and she used a lot of cosmetics. She colored her fingernails with violet fingernail polish. When she walked in the classroom, every student could smell her perfume. Her hair stuck out and was dyed with different colors every week. I thought I didn't have anything in common with her, but I was wrong. I found out she was Vietnamese one night in the computer lab. First, we talked about class and homework, and I watched her try to debug a program. Then I began to talk to her about more personal subjects. The more I talked to her, the more I admired her. Oanh's mother had abandoned the family, and Oanh's father had become sad and useless. Oanh took care of her whole family. She was trying to get a bachelor's degree in computer science so she could help her family. Although her appearance was like a Vietnamese punk rocker, Oanh was a strong and responsible person. I have learned not to judge others from their appearance. I hope that in the future I can convince Oanh to give up her rock and roll hairstyle.

—Cong Khieu

1. Why did the writer's feelings about Oanh change? Has this ever happened to you?

   _____

   _____

   _____

   _____

2. Is Oanh a personal hero for the writer? Why or why not?

   _____

   _____

   _____

   _____

3. What did you notice or like about this student example?

   _____

   _____

   _____

   _____

4. What questions or suggestions do you have for the writer of "Vietnamese Punk Rocker"?

   _____

   _____

   _____

   _____

Write

Now you're ready to write. Write about the person you chose in Choose a Topic. Describe how this person looks and acts. Describe an event that helps the reader "get to know" the person. Tell how this person has influenced you. You can take the writing you've already begun in this chapter and expand on it for this assignment.

After You Write

Revise

Now have someone else read your writing so that you know what to add or take away. Remember that in this stage of the writing process, you are looking at ideas. Exchange your paper with a classmate, or give your paper to your teacher, your mentor, or a friend to evaluate by answering these questions:

Questions for Revision	Yes	No
1. Has the writer written about a person he or she admires? Notes:		

2. Has the writer described the person according to some of these categories?
    physical appearance
    actions/personality/behavior
Notes:		

3. Has the writer emphasized one quality about his or her personal hero? Notes:		
4. Does the writer tell a story or describe an incident that shows more about the person he or she admires? Notes:		
5. Has the writer explained how this person has influenced him or her? Notes:		
6. Would you like to know something else about the person? If yes, write down something the writer should add:		

Plan your revision by reading the checklist. Talk with your teacher or classmates about what you can do to improve this writing. Write some notes in case you choose to rewrite this paper later.

Edit

Now review your writing for correctness. Look at spelling, punctuation, and grammar. Read and respond to the following checklist alone; then exchange papers and ask a classmate to answer the following questions:

Questions for Editing	Yes	No
1. Does the writer use vocabulary and vocabulary chunks from this chapter correctly? Notes:		
2. Does the writer use past tense verbs correctly? Notes:		
3. Are there any grammar mistakes you want to point out? If yes, write what the writer should check:		

Correct any mistakes your classmate or teacher pointed out in the Editing Checklist. Now you are ready to place your writing in your Writing Portfolio. You may choose to rewrite it or expand it to a longer piece now or later.

PUTTING IT ALL TOGETHER

Use What You Have Learned

Write about another person you admire. This time, choose a famous person. Use what you learned in this chapter to make your writing interesting and correct. Refer to your teacher's or classmate's comments on your first draft. When you are finished, share your writing in class. Put your writing in your Writing Portfolio.

Test-Taking Tip

Practice writing answers to sample essay questions before the test. Make up your own questions, or work with another student, writing questions for each other. When answering sample essay questions, give yourself the same amount of time you will have during the actual test. Don't refer to your study materials when answering sample essay questions.

CHECK YOUR PROGRESS

On a scale of 1 to 5, rate how well you have mastered the goals set at the beginning of the chapter.

1 2 3 4 5   write about a person you admire.

1 2 3 4 5   find a mentor to help you in and out of school.

1 2 3 4 5   practice learning vocabulary in "chunks" so that you can use new words correctly right away.

1 2 3 4 5   learn when and how to use the past perfect tense.

1 2 3 4 5   learn specific language for an assignment to make your writing precise.

If you've given yourself a 3 or lower on any of these goals:

- visit the *Tapestry* web site for additional practice.

- ask your instructor for extra help.

- review the sections of the chapter that you found difficult.

- work with a partner or study group to further your progress.

"Our identities, who and what we are, how others see us, are greatly affected by the names we are called."

—Haig Bosmajian

Read the quotation. What does it mean? Do you agree that our names are very important? Write down a fact about your name; then share your ideas in class:

_____

_____

_____

_____

3

MY NAME IS . . .

Names give us an identity. Names are signs of our individuality. They reflect who we are. In this chapter, you will read and think about names and write about your own.

Setting Goals

In this chapter, you will practice writing about the origin, meaning, or associations of a name. Specifically, you will write about your name. You will choose specific information to include and explain. In order to do this, you will:

◈ learn when and how to use the passive voice.

◈ learn the names of classmates, teachers, and important people on campus and in your community.

◈ review the rules of capitalization.

◈ read as much as you can to improve your writing.

What additional goals do you have for this chapter? Write them here:

_____

_____

Think about the names of your family members and good friends. Are these names traditional or modern? How do people get their names? What are some naming customs in your native culture? Write down what you know about names and naming customs; then talk about them with a partner.

_____

_____

_____

_____

MEETING THE TOPIC

A.   B.   C.   D.   E.

> A name should be chosen as an act of liberation, of celebration, of intention.
>
> —ERICA JONG

Look at the photos, which show five people. Then read about how they got their names. Match the photos with what each of the people says about his or her name:

_____ 1. "My name is Vu Hoang Au. It means 'gold rain' in Vietnamese. When my father was young, he was very poor. He had hopes for me. One of them was that I would have plenty of money. That's how I got my name."

_____ 2. "I have two names: Jose Agustin. I really don't like either of them. If I had been able to choose my names, I would certainly have said 'no' to these two names. You see, a few days before I was born one of my mother's brothers was killed. So my whole family decided to call me Agustin after him. Jose was another uncle who had died in a traffic accident. They thought the combination of Jose Agustin was perfect. It sounded good, and it reminded everyone of the two uncles. I also have two

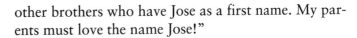
other brothers who have Jose as a first name. My parents must love the name Jose!"

_____ 3. "My name is Eileen, which is a typical Irish name, but when I was about two my dad gave me a nickname. He said that I was such a good little baby and I looked like a little doll. So he named me 'Dolly.' Even though I'm a teenager now, close friends and family members still use that nickname."

_____ 4. "My name is Maruca Antonia Beverly Jo Gomez. My mom made up Maruca. Antonia is a family name. Beverly Jo was my grandmother's name, and Gomez is my mom's last name. It's sort of a problem having such a long name because when I have to write it on a form at school or at the hospital, it's too long to fit in the boxes. My favorite part of the name is Beverly because although I never knew my grandmother, I learned many wonderful things about her. Actually, my long name is too much trouble for my brother. He calls me 'Pepper.' "

_____ 5. "Actually, until last month my name was Koo. My sister gave me that name when she couldn't pronounce my real name, and everyone has always called me Koo. Last month, when I turned 27, I finally decided to use my real name. So now all my friends and family members are trying to remember to call me Cornell. I don't know why my parents chose Cornell for me. My father chose my name; he must have had a special reason for naming me Cornell."

Give and get information about names. Talk with at least four students about their names. Fill in as much of the chart on the next page as you can with information you learn. Be prepared to give information about your name, too. Read the example to begin.

Name	What It Means	Where It Came From	How Person Feels About It
Vu Hoang Au	gold rain	father's hopes	I don't know

◆ Grammar You Can Use: Passive Voice

When you write about names, you will probably want to refer to your birth and how you got your name. Look at these two sentences:

> She *was born* in the year of the horse.

> She *was named* for her grandmother.

These expressions, *was born* and *was named*, require putting the verb in the **passive** rather than the usual **active** voice. The passive voice indicates that the subject is the **receiver**, not the **doer**, of the action. Verbs in the passive voice follow the subject and are made up of a form of *to be* and the past participle. Here's the formula:

SUBJECT + *TO BE* + PAST PARTICIPLE

Practice using the passive voice by writing answers to these questions:

1. Where were you born?

   _____

   _____

2. What was happening in the world when you were born?

   _____

   _____

3. Were you named for a special person?

   _____

   _____

4. There are three prepositions you can use after *to be named: for, by,* and *after*. They have different meanings. Match the phrase on the left with its correct meaning on the right:

I was named for my aunt.	My aunt gave me my name.
I was named by my aunt.	I have my aunt's name.
I was named after my aunt.	I have my aunt's name.

Which two expressions have the same meaning?

Freewrite

You've had a chance to learn about some people's names and talk about them with your classmates. Now you have a chance to begin writing about your name: how you got it, what it means, or how you feel about it. Write as much as you can for ten minutes without stopping. Remember that the purpose of freewriting is to get your ideas on paper. You will use some of these ideas for the writing assignment in this chapter. You can go back to develop and correct your writing later.

TUNING IN: "Married Names"

The CNN video you will watch describes the names women choose when they get married. What is the custom for women getting married in your native culture? Do they keep their names, take the name of their husband, or do both? Watch the video; then answer the following questions. Read the questions first in order to focus your listening.

1. How does Deletha, the wife of Joseph Coles III, write her name?

   a. Deletha Coles III

   b. Deletha Morrow Coles

   c. Deletha Morrow-Coles

2. What are two reasons why women keep their maiden name?

   a. _____

   b. _____

3. What percentage of women approve of keeping one's maiden name?

   a. 10%   b. 50.8%   c. 100%

© CNN

Do you or don't you take his name?

4. What percentage of women actually keep their maiden name?

   a. 10%

   b. 50.8%

   c. 00%

5. What did Bert Stinson do when he got married?

   a. He took his wife's name.

   b. He kept his name.

   c. He combined his name and his wife's name.

ACADEMIC POWER STRATEGY

Learn the names of your classmates, teachers, and important people on campus and in your community. Knowing the names of people in your school community can help you make friends and get assistance when you need it. Calling these people by their correct names shows respect and is an important social skill. In general, call people your own age by their first names: *Ellen, Juan, Frederique.* Address your teachers and people you are meeting for the first time more formally. Use a title and their last name: *Dr. Schmidt, Mr. Lammers, Ms. Morton, Mrs. Parrish.*

Apply the Strategy

Complete the following chart by writing the names of people in your school community. Work with a classmate to identify people and to decide how to address them correctly.

WHAT'S THE PERSON'S NAME?

HOW SHOULD THIS PERSON BE ADDRESSED?

Friends:

_____   _____

_____   _____

Teachers:

_____   _____

_____   _____

Other people I should know:

_____   _____

_____   _____

EXPANDING YOUR LANGUAGE

◊Vocabulary Check

Members of a tribe in Australia choose new names when they feel ready for one. They keep their birth names until they are five or six. Then they choose a new name based on talent or interest. They have a party to declare their new names. Their new names help others see them in a new way.

You will see the following vocabulary when you read about names in this chapter. Check the words and expressions you already know. Find meanings for words that are new and add them to your Vocabulary Log.

_____ confusion   _____ to be obvious

_____ customs   _____ to be stuck with

_____ decade   _____ to blame

_____ gender   _____ to follow tradition

_____ individuality   _____ to insist

_____ mistakenly   _____ to regret

_____ nickname   _____ to tease

_____ old-fashioned   _____ to threaten

_____ origin   _____ to track

_____ surname

◆**Vocabulary Tip**

Different Forms of the Same Word

You can increase your vocabulary for writing by learning how to take a word and use it in several ways. For example, *mistakenly* is an adverb, and it means that an action or event happened which was wrong. *Mistake* is a noun with the same meaning. *Mistaken* is an adjective. Use your knowledge of the meaning of one word to make more words.

1. Make more words from those in the list below. Work with a partner.

    individuality (noun)

        (adverb) _____

        (another noun) _____

    threaten (verb)

        (noun) _____

    origin (noun)

        (adjective) _____

2. Go back to the Freewrite you did in the previous section. Add to what you wrote by including sentences with one or more words from the list above.

◆**Vocabulary Building**

1. Match the words on the left to those on the right with the closest meanings.

customs	mixed-up situation
mistakenly	to make fun of
to follow tradition	sex
to blame	ceremonies
gender	to be clear
to tease	to feel sorry about
to be obvious	to be old-fashioned
confusion	to charge for wrongdoing
to regret	wrongly

2. Practice using the vocabulary from this chapter by writing short answers to these questions:

a. Do you have a **nickname**? How did you get it? Who calls you by your nickname?

_____

_____

b. People from the Middle East can **track** their heritage easily because of their naming **customs**. Children are given their father's first name. Are there naming customs in your native culture that have advantages?

_____

_____

c. Has anyone ever **teased** you about your name? What did he or she say?

_____

_____

d. What is a name you would hate **to be stuck with**? Why?

_____

_____

LANGUAGE LEARNING STRATEGY

Use capital letters correctly when writing about names. Including information about names in your writing requires paying special attention to capitalization rules. Review these rules:

1. **Use capital letters for:**

   • the first word in every sentence:

   The poet e e cummings was famous for his lack of capital letters.

(continued on next page)

- names of people and places:

    Cummings was born in Cambridge, Massachusetts, and attended Harvard University.

- titles and words like *mother, father, uncle* when they are used as titles:

    His books of poetry had such titles as <u>Tulips and Chimneys, Is 5</u>, *and* <u>No Thanks.</u>

- names of particular sections of a country or continent:

    Cummings' rebellious spirit and independent style of thinking was not common in traditional New England.

- names of organizations, associations, or teams:

    Cummings' <u>Poems: 1923–1954</u> *won a special prize from the National Book Awards Committee.*

- abbreviations of titles and organizations:

    Mr. Cummings was also known for his creative punctuation.

- races, nationalities, languages, and religions:

    All of Cummings' work was in playful and amusing English.

- nouns or pronouns that refer to a Supreme Being:

    It is not clear whether Cummings worshipped God, Allah, Buddha, or Jehovah.

2. **Don't use capital letters for:**

- fields of study (but do capitalize a specific course name):

    You probably won't learn about e e cummings if you study history, but you will study his poetry in British Literature 34C.

- seasons of the year (but do capitalize days of the week and months of the year):

  Janine read poems from Cummings' 95 Poems in February last year, during the winter break.

- words that indicate direction or position (but do capitalize names of particular regions):

  Cummings spent most of his life in the Northeast. We don't know if he ever traveled west.

Apply the Strategy

Practice applying the rules of capitalization by reading the following paragraph and putting capital letters where they belong.

in africa, children are the carriers of the future. it is the naming of each child that begins to establish his or her personal identity. therefore, the naming ceremony is an important occasion for all africans. it happens seven to ten days after the birth of the african child and takes place at the home of the mother and father. grandparents, aunts, uncles, and cousins are present. in west africa, most children have names that mark the day of the week on which they were born. for example, the akan people name a boy born on saturday *kwame*. they name a girl *ama*. west african names can also reflect the time of year of the birth, personal qualities the parents hope for in the child, or thanks to god. if a child comes during a time of planting, he will get a name meaning "planting" or "growing." the yoruba name "olufunmilayo" means "god gives me joy." it expresses the parents' hope for a happy child and great thanks to god.

READING FOR WRITING

Reading is a great way to improve your writing. You will read two selections on names. The first selection is an article about the new ways in which parents in the United States are giving names to their children. The second selection is about problems two people have with their names.

◀ Getting Ready to Read

Before you read, answer these questions:

- What is a person's first name? How is this different than his or her last name?

- What do you know about naming customs in the U.S. and Canada? Are naming customs in your native culture similar?

- Do people in your native culture ever "break the rules" for naming and do something completely different?

◀ Read

Reading 1: A Confusion of Last Names

1 Until the 1960s, almost everyone in the U.S. **followed tradition** and gave all the children in the same family the same last name—or **surname**, as it is called. But during the 60's, young parents began giving their children strange names—names like Moonglow, Eternal Peace, and Sunshine. Some states passed laws controlling the names that parents could use. But after a court case in 1981, a federal judge ruled that parents are free to give any surname they wish to their children.

2   So, for the last few **decades,** more parents are not giving their children the family's surname. Some mothers **insist** that while it's OK for a boy to have the father's family name, a girl should have the mother's family name. Thus, Philip Gaylord and Pam Zimmitti

Can names influence what we choose to do in life? Look at these names and professions: Justin Tune, musician in New Jersey; Kuhl Brieze, weather expert in Washington, D.C.; Lacy Leon Toothman, dentist in California.

could be brother and sister. Some parents think that using the family surname is **old-fashioned** and boring. One couple gave their son the last name Sue because they like the Johnny Cash song, "A Boy Named Sue." And finally, some parents think that giving their children different surnames is just a "neat thing to do." So the first son of a New York family has the last name Washington-Lincoln after the two famous presidents. The daughter has the last name Anthony-Tubman after two women who fought for women's rights.

3   This change in naming **customs** presents two problems. First, if each person in the family has a different last name, family records will be very **confused.** It will be hard to **track** a person's family, and record-keeping will be difficult. Second, some psychologists are afraid that different surnames will **threaten** family unity. Since names have an important effect on one's identity, they think brothers and sisters will not feel connected if they have different last names.

4   So this problem of names will get worse as new and different last names increase. Get ready to meet Welcome Baby Darling, sister of Aren't We Glad You're Here and It's About Time.

—adapted from *Current Scene*

◆ After You Read

1. The reading selection describes a problem with new customs in giving last names. Do you agree that it's a problem? Why or why not?

_____

_____

2. What are three reasons parents have chosen *not* to give their children the same last name?

REASON 1	REASON 2	REASON 3
_____	_____	_____
_____	_____	_____

3. What two problems result when parents give their children different last names?

PROBLEM 1	PROBLEM 2
_____	_____
_____	_____

4. Do all family members in your native culture have the same sur-name? If not, is this a problem?

_____

_____

5. If you could rename yourself or one of your children, what new name would you choose? Why?

_____

_____

Getting Ready to Read

Before you read, answer these questions:

- What are some unusual names you've heard about?

- What do you think are the three worst names to give a child? Why?

- What would you do if you were ashamed or embarrassed by your name?

It probably doesn't surprise you to learn that not everyone is happy with his or her name. In fact, ask people to talk about their names and you may hear some sad stories.

Read

Reading 2: Why Me?

Lorinda Gagnon:

I was the first child in the family. My mother couldn't decide between Lori and Linda, so she named me Lorinda. I have **regretted** her decision ever since. When I first went to school, I was **mistakenly** called Durinda, Burinda, or Mirinda. To make matters worse, my mother's nickname for me was Rini, which led to my close friends and family's favorite song to me: "Rin Tin Tin[1] sat on a pin." Then my teachers started calling me Laurainda. Now I automatically grit my teeth[2] when I meet a new person. "That's Lorinda," I say, "L-O-R-I-N-D-A!" Jane Smith, you don't know how lucky you are!

[1]**Rin Tin Tin:** dog movie star from the 1950s

[2]**grit my teeth:** stiffen one's jaw from stress

Terry T. Perry:

Mom blames Dad. Dad blames Mom. Whoever's to **blame,** I'm stuck with Terry T. Perry. There are three problems. The first is **obvious.** Everyone teases me all the time. The second problem is worse. My name has no **gender.** That means I get mail to Miss, Ms., Mrs., and Mr. Perry. The third problem is spelling. The variations are endless: Terrie Perrie, Terry Perri, Terri Pare. Some people insist my real name is Terrence. It's not easy. And if you're wondering about my middle name, don't ask. I'll never tell you anyway. I have enough problems with my first and last names.

—adapted from *Names, Names, Names*

◀ After You Read

> **Kris Freeman changed her name to Kris Freewoman when she moved out of her father's house.**

1. Why are Lorinda and Terry unhappy with their names?

   _____

   _____

   _____

2. Think of one person you know who is unhappy with his or her name. Why is this person unhappy?

   _____

   _____

   _____

3. Lorinda and Terry explain what they dislike about their names. Is there anything you find good about their names? Write two advantages of their names.

   _____

   _____

   _____

4. Write a short letter to Lorinda or Terry and propose a solution to their name problems.

   Dear _____,

   _____

   _____

   _____

   Sincerely,

   _____

LANGUAGE LEARNING STRATEGY

Read as much as you can to improve your writing. Reading will help you write better. By reading as much as you can, you can get ideas for your writing, learn new words and phrases, and observe how language is used correctly. Read magazines, posters, signs, articles on the internet, newspapers, and books. Good writers are good readers.

Apply the Strategy

Read something related to the topic of this chapter. Report to the class on what you read. Here are some suggestions:

- a poem by e e cummings

- a news article about popular names

- an advertisement about a product with an unusual name

- an explanation about how something got its name

- a map with common street names

FROM READING TO WRITING

There are lots of ways to write about names. One way is for a writer to write about the meaning of his or her own name. Another way is to explain how a writer got his or her name. A writer can describe the friends, famous people, or relatives he or she was named by or after. Writers can also write about their feelings about their names. Finally, they can give themselves new names and explain how these new names reflect who they are. Take notes on your name in the chart below. Fill in as much information as you can. Add more information about your name in the last row of the chart. You will use this writing for the assignment in this chapter.

MY NAME: _____

What it means _____

How I got it _____

Who I was named after _____

How I feel about it   _____

If I could have a new name . . .   _____

                                       _____

Getting Ready to Write

Writing About Names

Writing about names involves making choices about what kinds of information you will include. Follow these tips as you get ready to write.

Choose From Different Kinds of Information

When you write about your name, there are several topics you can write about. Choose two or three kinds of information to explain and develop. Look at the kinds of information you can include:

- what the name means
- how you got the name
- advantages and disadvantages of the name
- how you feel about the name
- how other people feel about the name
- associations with the name

Develop a paragraph around each different topic.

Practice Write at least one paragraph on one of the topics listed above. Expand and develop the writing you have already begun in this chapter.

Expand Your Writing with Reasons and Examples

When you write about your name, explain and develop your writing by giving reasons and examples. Reasons answer the question *Why?* Look at this example:

> My name is Margarita. When I was a child, I didn't like my name because somebody once told me it was associated with flirtatious women. **I was a very shy girl, and I didn't like this association.** I also didn't like the English translation for my name. So I decided to change my name to Peggy. **I wanted to be an astronaut, so I chose the name of a girl from a TV series about a space trip.**

Practice Add reasons and examples to the paragraph you developed in the previous exercise.

Add Your Opinion

You can make your writing interesting by including your opinion about your name. This tells the reader about you. Explain why you like or dislike your name. Describe a funny or embarrassing incident associated with your name.

Practice Add your opinion to the paragraph you have developed in this section.

Choose a Topic

Now choose the topic of this chapter's writing assignment. If you don't have enough information on one of the topics listed below for an essay, combine two or more topics.

- your name
- how you got your name
- associations with your name
- your nickname
- problems with your name
- a new name you want to give yourself
- a ceremony associated with naming

Plan Your Writing

Answer these questions to organize the information about your name:

1. How will you begin writing about your name? What topic or topics did you choose to write about?

   _____

   _____

2. What reasons will you include to explain and develop your writing?

   _____

   _____

3. What examples will you write about?

_____

_____

4. How will you end your writing? What conclusions about your name will you add?

_____

_____

Study a Student Example

Read the following essay that a college student wrote.

My Name

1   My name is Ming-che Wu. When I introduce myself to foreign people, I use Ming-che even though it's Chinese. I don't want to use an American name like Tom, David, or John because I'm a traditional Chinese person. It's a little difficult for foreign people to pronounce *che*, so I prefer to use Ming as my English name. It's a name people can remember easily. In Chinese, Ming means bright, smart, intelligent. I like my name because it gives me a reason to become a philosopher.

2   There are a few problems with my name because it is very common in my country. Once, in senior high, a classmate had exactly the same name as me. The teachers didn't know how to distinguish between us. So when asking us to answer questions, one teacher identified us by using our school numbers. The school always confused us. Sometimes they thought I had filled out forms when the other Ming-che Wu had done it. Finally, my classmates started calling me "Big Ming" to mark me because I was taller than the other one. We became very good friends because of our common name. I like my name a lot even though it is so common in Taiwan. If I had a chance to choose a new name, I'd choose the same name that I have now.

—Ming-che Wu

1. What are two problems with Ming-che's name?

   a. _____

   b. _____

2. What does the writer like about his name?

   _____

   _____

3. What did you notice or like about this student example?

   _____

   _____

4. What question or suggestion do you have for this writer?

   _____

   _____

Write

Now you're ready to write. Write about your name. Explain its meaning, origin, associations, or advantages (and disadvantages). Include reasons and examples that help the reader understand your point of view. You can expand on the writing you've already begun in this chapter or start something new.

After You Write

Revise

Now have someone else read your writing so that you know what to add or take away. At this stage of the writing process, you are looking at ideas. Exchange your paper with a classmate, or give your paper to your teacher, your mentor, or a friend to evaluate by answering these questions:

Questions for Revision	Yes	No
1. Has the writer selected two or three kinds of information to explain about his or her name or a naming custom? Notes:		
2. Does the writer include reasons to develop or explain his or her opinion? Notes:		

Questions for Revision	Yes	No
3. Does the writer include examples? Notes:		
4. Are there any comments or recommendations you can make to improve this paper? If yes, write here something the writer could do:		

Plan your revision by reading the checklist. Talk with your teacher or classmates about what you can do to improve this essay. Write some notes in case you choose to rewrite this paper later.

Edit

Now review your writing for correctness. Look at spelling, punctuation, and grammar. Read and respond to this checklist alone; then exchange papers and ask a classmate to answer these questions:

Questions for Editing	Yes	No
1. Does the writer use vocabulary from this chapter correctly? Notes:		
2. Does the writer use capital letters correctly? Notes:		
3. Does the writer use passive voice correctly? Notes:		
4. Are there any grammar mistakes you want to point out? If yes, write what the writer should check:		

Correct any mistakes that you found or that your classmate or teacher pointed out in the Editing Checklist. Now you are ready to place your writing in your Writing Portfolio. You may choose to rewrite it or expand it to a longer piece now or later.

PUTTING IT ALL TOGETHER

Interview two people outside of class about their names. Start with the following questions, and then add some of your own:

1. What is your name? What does it mean?

2. Where did your name come from?

3. Who named you?

4. How do feel about your name? If you could change your name, what would your new name be?

View the film *Roots,* based on the book by Alex Haley. Watch for the naming ceremony at the beginning of the movie. Write your opinion about the ceremony.

Test-Taking Tip

Create a calm atmosphere for yourself before a test. Leave plenty of time to get to the test and relax on campus immediately beforehand. Perhaps sit with a newspaper and a cup of coffee or listen to some of your favorite music on a portable music player. Avoid conversations with other students about the test and don't study in the last hour before the test—doing these things will only cause anxiety.

CHECK YOUR PROGRESS

On a scale of 1 to 5, rate how well you have mastered the goals set at the beginning of the chapter:

1 2 3 4 5   write about your name.

1 2 3 4 5   learn when and how to use the passive voice.

1 2 3 4 5   learn the names of classmates, teachers, and important people on campus and in your community.

1 2 3 4 5   review the rules of capitalization.

1 2 3 4 5   read as much as you can to improve your writing.

If you've given yourself a 3 or lower on any of these goals:

- visit the *Tapestry* web site for additional practice.
- ask your instructor for extra help.
- review the sections of the chapter that you found difficult.
- work with a partner or study group to further your progress.

"I hear and I forget, I see and I remember, I do and I understand."

—Chinese proverb

Read the proverb. What is the difference between *remember* and *understand*? Which is more important? Do people all learn in the same way? Write down a few of your ideas about what the proverb means; then share your ideas in class:

_____

_____

_____

_____

4

HOW DID YOU LEARN THAT?

People take in information through their five senses: sight, hearing, touch, smell, and taste. We use sight, hearing, and touch most frequently. Knowing more about how you take in information can help you learn, remember, and (as the proverb suggests) understand more. In this chapter, you will think and read about different learning styles and write about how you learn best.

Setting Goals

In this chapter, you will practice writing to explain and justify. Specifically, you will write about how you learn best. You will explain your learning style and give examples to show how it works for you. In order to do this, you will:

◈ become aware of your learning style.

◈ explore learning resources on campus.

◈ learn stems and affixes to expand your vocabulary for writing.

◈ use *make* and *do* correctly in your writing.

What additional goals do you have for this chapter? Write them here:

_____

_____

◆**Getting Started**

Think about a time when your learning was really successful. What were you trying to learn? Where were you? Who were you with? What did the teacher do? What activities were included? Write down what you remember from this learning experience; then talk about it with a partner.

_____

_____

_____

_____

MEETING THE TOPIC

Look at the picture which shows people learning in different ways. Describe what each of the people is doing to learn.

1. <u>The girl is touching the statue.</u> _____

2. _____

3. _____

4. _____

5. _____

6. _____

LANGUAGE LEARNING STRATEGY

Be aware of your style of learning when learning something new. If you know what works and doesn't work for you when learning new material, you can save time and do better in school. Making the right choices about how to study based on your learning style will help you learn more effectively.

Apply the Strategy

Think about your learning style as you read the following chart. First look at column 1. Circle the method you prefer to use (A, B, or C) in column 2, or think of another possible method (D) and write it in the chart. When you have completed the chart, share the methods you've circled with two classmates. Did you have similar or different answers?

Column 1 What do you want to learn?	Column 2 How would you try to learn it?			
	A	**B**	**C**	**D**
a musical selection to play on the piano	read the notes	listen to a recording of the selection	try to find the right keys on the piano and play the piece	another way:
an expression in English that's really difficult to pronounce	read the words	listen to someone else say it	write the words	another way:
the meaning of the word *stretch*	look it up in the dictionary	ask someone to tell you	to remember the meaning, extend your arms and legs	another way:
how to greet a person for the first time	read information on social customs	listen to someone else tell you how to do it	practice by imitating another person	another way:

(continued on next page)

Look at the pattern of your circles. Were most of them in one column?

- If your circles were mostly in Column 2A, you may be a person who learns best by **seeing** what you need to learn. This type of person is a **visual** learner.

- If your circles were mostly in Column 2B, you may be a person who learns best by **hearing** what you need to learn. This type of person is an **auditory** learner.

- If your circles were mostly in Column 2C, you may be a person who learns best by **doing** what you need to learn. This type of person is a **kinesthetic** or hands-on learner.

If your circles were in different columns, you may prefer a combination of learning styles.

Freewrite

You've had a chance to look at some photos of people learning in different ways, listen to your classmates talk about how they learn, and think about some of your own successful learning experiences. Here's your chance to freewrite about the way that you learn best. Write for ten minutes without stopping.

TUNING IN: "Learning at Home"

© CNN

Learning at Home

People have distinct learning styles. They also have preferences about the social settings where they learn. Some people like large classes and large schools. Others prefer small classes and small schools. Still others prefer learning at home rather than going to school. The CNN video you will watch shows one family that has chosen learning at home. Are there many "home schoolers" in your native culture? Would you like to be "home schooled"? What do you think are the advantages of studying at home? What are the disadvantages? Read the following questions first. Then watch the video and answer the questions.

1. Where do the Hughes children go to school?

   a. in the basement of their home

   b. at the neighborhood school

   c. at the local library

2. How many students in the United States go to school at home?

   a. half a million

   b. one million

   c. 100 million

3. Why does Lisa Hughes choose to teach her children at home school?

   a. The local school is crowded.

   b. The local school is dangerous.

   c. The local school is far from home.

4. According to the video, what is one advantage of home schooling?

   a. Families can control the quality of their children's education.

   b. Sometimes students miss their friends.

   c. Families always have all the books they need.

5. According to the video, what is one disadvantage to home schooling?

   a. Children learn social skills at home.

   b. Home school is very convenient.

   c. Parents are not always prepared to be teachers.

6. Which learning style do you think would be most successful with home schooling? Discuss answers to this question with your classmates before you write an answer. Give reasons to support your answer.

> The home schooling movement has been active in the United States for over 25 years. There are magazines, organizations, publishers, and support groups for parents who want their children educated at home.

ACADEMIC POWER STRATEGY

Explore learning resources on campus. Many college campuses have facilities for students to learn new material in different ways. For example, students at some schools can study languages in a language laboratory, view videos in the video library, use a computer in the computer laboratory, or meet with people who can help in the tutoring center. Learn the resources at your school to help you in completing all your assignments successfully.

(continued on next page)

Apply the Strategy

Complete the following chart about learning resources on campus. If your campus does not have these learning resources, check to see if you can find them at a school nearby or somewhere else in the community. Add another learning resource to the chart if you can.

Learning Resource	Where is it?	When is it open?	What can I find there?
language laboratory			
video library			
computer laboratory			
tutoring center			

EXPANDING YOUR LANGUAGE

**Vocabulary Check**

Study the following vocabulary for writing about learning styles. You will see these words in the reading selections, and you will want to use them for the writing assignment. Check the words and expressions you already know. Find meanings for words that are new to you and add them to your Vocabulary Log.

_____ analytic	_____ relational
_____ approach	_____ sensory
_____ auditory	_____ significant
_____ competitive	_____ strategies
_____ cooperation	_____ to be dependent on
_____ kinesthetic	_____ to be distracted by
_____ pattern	_____ to result in
_____ perceptual	_____ under the supervision of
_____ physical	_____ visual
_____ preference	

LANGUAGE LEARNING STRATEGY

Learn stems and affixes to expand your vocabulary for writing. One way to increase your vocabulary is to learn the parts of words. There are three parts: **prefixes, suffixes,** and **stems.** Prefixes and suffixes are called **affixes.** By knowing the function and meaning of word parts, you can understand what words mean and you can create new words.

• **Prefixes** come at the beginning of words:

**intersection, mistake, multilingual**

When I learned to drive, I studied diagrams of where to stop at **intersections.** The diagrams were **multilingual.**

• **Suffixes** come at the end of words:

**driver, careful, ambitious**

I wanted to be a very careful **driver,** so I read the books for many hours.

(continued on next page)

- **Stems** are the basic part of the word. Prefixes and suffixes are attached to stems:

  auto, dict, meter

  *I studied so hard that all my friends pre**dict**ed I would be an excellent driver. When I passed the driving test, I decided I earned a new **auto**mobile.*

Prefixes affect the meaning of a stem, and suffixes change the part of speech.

Apply the Strategy

Study some common word parts and their meanings in the chart below.

PREFIXES	Meaning	STEMS	Meaning	SUFFIXES	Meaning (Part of Speech)
non-	not	**auto**	self	**-able**	capable of (adj.)
re-	again	**bio**	life	**-er**	one who (noun)
inter-	between	**dict**	say	**-ly**	in this way (adverb)
multi-	many	**geo**	earth	**-ful**	full of (adj.)
un-	not	**graph**	write	**-al**	related to (adj.)
mis-	wrong	**logy**	study	**-tion**	condition (noun)
vis-	see, sight	**meter**	measure	**-ory**	related to (adj.)

1. Identify the parts in the boldfaced words in the following paragraph. Underline <u>prefixes</u>, circle (stems) and put a wavy line under suffixes.

   I learned to cook from my mother's **dictation**. She was a great **teacher**. I guess it didn't hurt that I was an **auditory learner**. Mother read the **instructions**; I listened **carefully**, and did what she said. For a **beginner**, I was a **remarkable** cook. I made a **mistake** only once. I used salt instead of sugar for a holiday cake. I thought the cake was **acceptable**, so I served it. All the guests left **quickly** after eating the cake. No one ever asked me to **remake** that cake. I wonder why.

2. What is the writer's learning style?

_____

_____

_____

3. Use some of the words from the chart and some of your own words in sentences. Write short answers to the following questions. Share what you write in class.

a. geology   biology   anthropology   astrology   meteorology

Which of these fields of science interest you? Have you studied any of them?

_____

_____

_____

b. dangerous   rapidly   fearful   cautious

Do you know how to swim? How did you learn? Where do you like to swim?

_____

_____

_____

c. patiently   carefully   kilometer   bike rider

How did you learn to ride a bicycle? Who taught you?

_____

_____

_____

d. graphics   multimedia   computer   helpful   application

Do you use a computer for school? How useful is it? What do you do best on the computer?

_____

_____

_____

◆**Vocabulary Building**

1. Match the words on the left to those on the right with the closest meanings.

determine	idea
kinesthetic	together
interaction	learn by heart
preference	physical
cooperative	influence
memorize	important
concept	conversation
significant	first choice

2. Practice using the vocabulary from this chapter by writing short answers to these questions:

   a. When you are studying, what **are you distracted by**? What do you do to avoid this distraction?

   _____

   _____

   b. Were you **dependent on someone** to help you enroll in this class? How did this person help you?

   _____

   _____

   c. What have you done recently **under the supervision of another person**? Has it been easy or difficult to work under someone's supervision?

   _____

   _____

   d. What have you done recently **in cooperation with another person**? Has it been easier or more difficult to work closely with someone else?

   _____

   _____

READING FOR WRITING

The two reading selections here are about culture and learning styles. They will help you think about how you learn best. You can use the ideas and language from these reading selections in your writing assignment. The first selection is from a book preparing teachers to work with groups of students from different language backgrounds and cultures. The second selection is from a textbook for native speakers.

Getting Ready to Read

Before you read, answer these questions:

- What two pieces of advice would you give to a beginning teacher working with people from your native culture?

- Which affects learning most, culture or learning styles?

Read

Reading 1: Culture and Learning Styles

Culture determines what kind of thinking is important and what kind is devalued. Learners use the language, tools, and practices of their culture to learn concepts. Although students have individual learning styles, these learning styles are often combined with cultural values. For example, Navajo children often learn first by observing and listening. Then, when ready, they continue learning on their own in **cooperation** with and **under the supervision of** an adult. In this way, the children learn all the skills they need. Navajo children speak very little during this process. In contrast, many African-American children learn effectively by acting and performing. They like classroom activities such as oral presentations, roleplays, and dramatic performances. Lots of talking is useful for these students. Another way of learning is through reading and writing. Asian students generally need writing to support their learning, and therefore do well in classes where there is lots of reading and writing. It is common to see Japanese students trace the spelling of words they have heard. They are more comfortable seeing new material than hearing it. Koreans are believed to be the most **visual** learners. So, although learning styles significantly determine how a person takes in new material, one's culture also influences how he learns.

—adapted from Diaz-Rico and Weed,
*The Crosscultural, Language, and
Academic Development Handbook*

After You Read

1. The reading selection describes how both culture and learning style influence a person. Think about your own learning. Is it influenced more by culture or by learning style? Fill in the culture and learning style "barometers"; then share your work with a classmate. Begin at the bottom and stop at the level that matches the influence your culture and learning style have had on your learning.

My native culture:		My learning style:
	has had a significant influence on my learning	
	has had a moderate influence on my learning	
	has had very little influence on my learning	

2. Complete the table according to information from the reading.

NATIVE CULTURE	PREFERRED LEARNING STYLE	EXAMPLE
Navajo		
African American		
Korean		

3. Pretend that someone is coming to your native country to teach. What should this person know about how students learn best?

_____

_____

Getting Ready to Read

Before you read, answer these questions:

• Are you a visual, auditory, or kinesthetic learner?

• Do students from your native culture prefer one style of learning? If yes, which one?

• Which learning style does "hands-on" refer to?

Read

Reading 2: Language Learning, Learning Styles, and Culture

1   Language learning styles are the general **approaches** students use to learn a new language and the same styles they use in learning many other subjects and solving various problems. There are four ways of explaining language learning styles. We will look at only one way here: **sensory preferences.** Students' preferences for a particular sensory approach result in **significant** differences between language learners. Sensory preferences refer to the **physical** and **perceptual** learning channels with which students are most comfortable. The three major sensory preferences are visual, **auditory,** and hands-on (movement and touch).

2   Visual students need to see what is asked of them. They like to read, look at pictures, and they are good at noticing visual details. They can also be distracted by visual details: a new sign, a bird outside the window, or a person walking past the classroom. For them, lectures, conversation, and oral directions without any visual support can be confusing or difficult to understand.

3   Auditory learners, on the other hand, are comfortable without information presented visually. They learn most quickly from lectures, conversations, and oral directions. They do well with classroom activities that involve talking, roleplaying, and singing. They remember names, song lyrics, and pronunciation **patterns** easily. They can have difficulty with written work.

4   Hands-on students like to be physically active and work with objects, build projects, and move around. They have difficulty sitting still for long periods of time. They learn best through their muscles and often tap or drum when still. Hands-on learners touch objects they walk past and use lots of facial expressions and gestures when they talk.

5   The sensory preferences of different learners can result in a class of students with completely different strengths and weaknesses. A teacher who is aware of the different learning styles and includes activities that support all three types of learners is serving all students.

—adapted from Scarcella and Oxford,
The Tapestry of Language Learning

> We learn 10% of what we read, 20% of what we hear, 30% of what we see, 50% of what we see and hear, 70% of what we discuss, 80% of what we experience, and 95% of what we teach others.
>
> **—WILLIAM GLASSER**

After You Read

1. How would you explain learning styles to a friend? Write your explanation below:

_____

_____

_____

> . . . a teacher has an obligation to care about every student as a learner.
>
> —HERBERT KOHL

2. Describe one activity each of these students does very well:

   • a visual learner

   _____

   _____

   _____

   _____

   • an auditory learner

   _____

   _____

   _____

   _____

   • a kinesthetic learner

   _____

   _____

   _____

   _____

3. Describe one activity each of these students **doesn't** do as well:

   • a visual learner

   _____

   _____

   _____

   _____

   • an auditory learner

   _____

   _____

   _____

   • a kinesthetic learner

   _____

   _____

   _____

   _____

4. What can happen in a class where a student is a kinesthetic, or hands-on, learner and all the activities are reading and writing?

_____

_____

_____

5. Imagine that you are going to teach a class. You want to include activities for all three kinds of learners: visual, auditory, and kinesthetic. Would the following activities be easiest for a visual, auditory, or kinesthetic learner? Check the appropriate box in the chart.

Activity	Visual	Auditory	Kinesthetic
1. Putting vocabulary words on flashcards.			
2. Performing a puppet show.			
3. Tracing in the air to learn the correct spelling of vocabulary words.			
4. Memorizing a poem.			
5. Using pictures to introduce vocabulary.			
6. Writing directions for every task.			
7. "Acting out" actions to learn verbs.			
8. Using different colors to indicate nouns, verbs, and adjectives.			
9. Teaching new vocabulary through a song.			

FROM READING TO WRITING

Keep track of your learning for a day. Take notes on the learning activities you do. Indicate whether the activities are directed at visual, auditory, or kinesthetic learners. Record your feelings and rate of success as you do the activities. Make a chart like the one on the next page. This will help you collect more information about your learning style.

Activity	Visual	Auditory	Kinesthetic	Feelings	Did You Learn?
Drew pictures of new words			✓	Confident	Yes

◇ **Grammar You Can Use: Using *Make* and *Do* Correctly**

Many students have trouble knowing when to use make and do in their writing. Do the following expressions go with *make* or *do*?

1. Match the *make* and *do* expressions below with their definitions.

DEFINITION	*MAKE* OR *DO* EXPRESSION
use	make a difference
wash dirty clothes	do the dishes
be clear	make up
pretend	do homework
complete assignments from class	make sense
agree to be friends again	make a decision
get along at a minimum level	make a contribution
give something to someone	make fun of someone
wash dirty dishes	make up something
invent	make use of
tease or mock another person	make believe
have an effect	do the laundry
choose	make do

2. The best way to learn *make* and *do* expressions is to memorize them. Memorize the expressions in the right column of the chart above according to your preferred learning style. A visual learner can memorize by making a poster of expressions and imagining the writing. An auditory learner might listen to a poem or song

to memorize expressions. A kinesthetic learner could do movements to match the meaning of the expressions.

3. Now test yourself. Complete the chart by putting the expressions in the correct column. Don't look back at the previous page. Check your answers with a classmate.

laundry	a contribution	fun of someone
sense	a decision	a difference
use of	up	dishes
homework	believe	do
up something		

Make	*Do*

Getting Ready to Write

Writing About Learning Styles

As you have seen in the reading selections, writing about learning styles involves making general statements about all learners and including specific examples about your own learning experiences or the experiences of others that you have read about or observed. Therefore, it is important to include examples in this type of writing. Follow these tips as you get ready to write.

Begin with a General Statement

Whether you are writing several paragraphs or an academic essay, you will want to begin with a general statement that tells the reader the main idea of your writing. This is called the **thesis statement.** Reread the general sentences from introductory paragraphs in the reading selections from this chapter:

- Culture determines what kind of thinking is important and what kind is devalued.

- Language learning styles are the general approaches students use to learn a new language and the same styles they use in learning many other subjects and solving various problems.

Practice Go back to the freewrite you did at the beginning of the chapter. Write a general statement expressing the main idea of this writing.

Include Lots of Specific Examples

When you write about learning styles, give lots of specific examples. Examples can be from your own experience or from your observations or reading. Examples show how general statements are true. Read the examples from readings in this chapter:

- Navajo children often learn first by observing and listening.
- Asian students generally need writing to support their learning.
- Visual students are good at noticing visual details.
- Hands-on students like to be physically active and work with objects, build projects, and move around.

Practice What specific examples can you use to support the general statement from your freewrite? Develop at least two specific examples.

Write an Effective Conclusion

The conclusion, or the final sentence or paragraph, restates the topic and pulls together the general statements and specific examples. Some writers save the most important ideas for the end in order to make a strong impression on their readers. Here are some concluding sentences from this chapter:

- So, although learning styles significantly determine how a person takes in new material, one's culture also influences how he learns.

- A teacher who is aware of the different learning styles and includes activities that support all three types of learners is serving all students.

Practice Now write one or more sentences that pull together the general statement and the specific examples.

Choose a Topic

Your assignment for this chapter is to write about your learning style. Choose from one of these options:

- Write about how you learn best.

- Write about someone else's learning style preference.

- If you can make a general statement, write about a group's learning style. This could be a cultural group, a specific-age group, or a family.

- Write a letter of advice to a new English teacher. Tell this person how to be an effective teacher by supporting all learning style preferences.

Plan Your Writing

Organize your information by taking notes in the chart. Follow the model of "Learning Styles" by Scarcella and Oxford. Put your most general information in the introduction, and make sure your general statement, or main idea, is the last sentence of the first paragraph. Plan your writing by answering these questions:

Introduction	Most general idea: What are different learning styles?	
Thesis Statement	Main idea: What kind of learner are you?	
Paragraph 1 *Topic Sentence*	What's one reason you know you're a (visual, auditory, kinesthetic) learner?	
Paragraph 2 *Topic Sentence*	What's a second reason you know you're a (visual, auditory, kinesthetic) learner?	
Paragraph 3 *Topic Sentence*	What's a third reason you know you're a (visual, auditory, kinesthetic) learner?	
Conclusion	How does your learning style relate to other activities?	

Study a Student Example

Read the following essay that a college student wrote; then answer the questions.

> **Those who try harder do better.**
>
> **—ALBERT ROSENFELD**

An Expert in Vocabulary

1 I am an eager student in all subjects thanks to my excellent teachers, my hard-working parents, and my dedicated sisters. When I don't understand something, I work very hard until I understand it. I have used lots of methods to learn vocabulary, and I have become my own best teacher.

2   I have tried to teach myself new words everywhere and all the time. First, when I was a child, I studied vocabulary in illustrated books for children. I looked at the pictures mostly and tried to the learn the spelling When someone read something to me, I often repeated the pronunciation of the new word. Even as a child I was an eager student.

3   As I got older, when I was in my teens, I could write and read better. During that time, I chose some good dictionaries and some good grammar books. I also had a dictionary of synonyms and antonyms. I also studied vocabulary in newspapers and magazines. I even studied vocabulary outside of school with my friends.

4   Now when I discover a new word which I don't know, I write and rewrite it and read and reread it many times until I learn the meaning and spelling by heart. Sometimes I get discouraged when I forget my vocabulary and it seems I am very stupid. Thanks to my teachers' help recently, I have learned some new and different methods of studying vocabulary. I am trying my best to learn a great deal of vocabulary now.

—Hinh Nguyen

1. This writer doesn't mention a particular learning style, but he refers to lots of learning methods. Which learning style do you think the writer prefers? Why?

2. How many specific examples did you find in this student example? Put an asterisk next to each example.

3. What did you notice or like about this student example?

4. What questions or suggestions do you have for the writer?

 Write

Now write an essay about your learning style. Include a general statement. Develop your writing through specific examples. Complete your writing with an effective conclusion. You may refer to the readings and use the writing you've done in this chapter to help you.

After You Write

Revise

Now have someone else read your writing so that you know what to add or take away. In this stage of the writing process, you are looking at ideas. Exchange your paper with a classmate or give your paper to your teacher, your mentor, or a friend to evaluate by answering these questions:

Questions for Revision	Yes	No
1. Has the writer presented the main idea in a general statement at the beginning of the writing? Notes:		
2. Does the writer include specific examples to help the reader understand? Notes:		
3. Are there enough examples? Indicate where an example could be added or made clearer. Notes:		
4. Has the writer finished with a conclusion that brings everything together? Notes:		
5. Are there any comments or recommendations you can make that might improve this paper? If yes, write here something the writer could do:		

Plan your revision by reading the checklist. Talk with your teacher or classmates about what you can do to improve this essay. Write some notes in case you choose to rewrite this paper later.

Edit

Now review your writing for correctness. Look at spelling, punctuation, and grammar. Read and respond to this checklist alone; then exchange papers and ask a classmate to answer these questions:

Questions for Editing	Yes	No
1. Has the writer used *make* and *do* expressions correctly? Notes:		
2. Has the writer used stems and affixes correctly? Notes:		
3. Has the writer used vocabulary from this chapter correctly? Notes:		
4. Are there any grammar mistakes you want to point out? If yes, write what the writer should check:		

Correct any mistakes your classmate or teacher pointed out in the Editing Checklist. Now you are ready to place your writing in your Writing Portfolio. You may choose to rewrite it or expand it to a longer piece now or later.

PUTTING IT ALL TOGETHER

Use What You Have Learned

- Think about a skill people generally learn outside of school. This could be cooking, swimming, bike riding, mountain climbing, gardening, training pets, or any other activity or hobby that interests you. Write about the best way to learn this skill. Use what you learned in this chapter to make your writing interesting and correct. Refer to your teacher's or classmate's comments on your first draft. When you are finished, put your writing in your Writing Portfolio.

- Be teacher for a day. Teach your class something new. Include activities for all three learning styles.

Test-Taking Tip

Before trying to answer a question, put it in your own words. The language of essay questions may, at first, seem very complicated and difficult. Rephrasing the question in your own words will simplify the question, make sure that you really understand the question before you try to answer it, and give you more confidence as you begin to write your answer.

CHECK YOUR PROGRESS

On a scale of 1 to 5, rate how well you have mastered the goals set at the beginning of the chapter:

1 2 3 4 5   write about how you learn best.

1 2 3 4 5   become aware of your learning style.

1 2 3 4 5   explore learning resources on campus.

1 2 3 4 5   learn stems and affixes to expand your vocabulary for writing.

1 2 3 4 5   use *make* and *do* correctly in your writing.

If you've given yourself a 3 or lower on any of these goals:

- visit the *Tapestry* web site for additional practice.
- ask your instructor for extra help.
- review the sections of the chapter that you found difficult.
- work with a partner or study group to further your progress.

"When everything in your life is uncertain, there's nothing quite like the clarity and precision of fresh snow and blue sky."

—Pam Houston

Read the quotation by Pam Houston. She describes the relationship between places and feelings. What do you think she means? Do you agree? Write about a place you know that makes you feel a certain way:

_____

_____

_____

_____

A PLACE IN THE WORLD

M any famous writers have described places where they have lived or visited. These places have inspired them to express important feelings. When you write about a place you know well, you may learn new things about yourself. In this chapter, you are going to describe a special place and tell the reader how it makes you feel.

Setting Goals

In this chapter, you will practice writing a description. Specifically, you will describe a place and explain how the place makes you feel. You will use descriptive adjectives and include specific details about places. In order to do this, you will:

◈ use a journal to connect your personal life to school assignments.

◈ guess the meanings of new words in context.

◈ practice using result clauses: *so* + adjective (*that*).

◈ memorize grammar structures.

What additional goals do you have for this chapter? Write them here:

_____

_____

◆ **Getting Started**

With a partner, brainstorm a list of special places: places that you go to relax or to be quiet. Talk about your favorite places. For each place, think about these things:

- What does it look like?
- What do you usually do in this place?
- How does this place make you feel?

Write down one or two ideas:

_____

_____

_____

MEETING THE TOPIC

Look at the photos of places. Try to guess what each place is. Then think of two or three words that describe each place. Write your words on the lines below.

A.

B.

C.

D.

E.

F.

A. _____

B. _____

C. _____

D. _____

E. _____

F. _____

Give and get vocabulary that describes the places in the photos on page 104. Complete the following chart. For each word or expression that you get from a classmate, give a new word or expression. After you share your vocabulary, move on to a new classmate. Try to get as many new words and expressions that describe places as you can.

Place:	Photo A	Photo B	Photo C	Photo D	Photo E	Photo F
D V						peaceful
e o						
s c						
c a						
r b						
i u						
p l						
t a						
i r						
v y						
e						

ACADEMIC POWER STRATEGY

Apply the Strategy

Keep a journal to connect your personal life to school assignments. One way to use your journal is to write about things you see, do, hear, or talk about with friends and at school. This will give you ideas for essays and other school assignments and make you a better writer.

Use your freewrite assignment to write a journal entry about a place.

Freewrite

You've had a chance to look, listen, and talk. Now connect your ideas in writing. In your journal, write about one of your favorite places. Describe it. It can be indoors or outdoors—a place where you work, play, study, or do nothing. It can be the place you described at the beginning of this chapter, or you may choose to write about a different place. You can write notes or sentences, or make a list. Write as quickly as you can. Don't worry about grammar or spelling; just get your ideas on paper.

TUNING IN: "Hawaiian Petroglyphs"

The CNN video you will watch is about a special place in Hawaii, the Puako Petroglyph Archaeological District. Here, ancient Hawaiians carved religious pictures into rocks. Read the following questions first. Then watch the video and answer the questions.

1. Why is this place special?

   a. It has a lot of flowers.

   b. It has a lot of power.

   c. It has no power.

2. Describe how this place makes the man feel.

   a. It gives him goosebumps (or "chicken skin").

   b. It makes him tired.

   c. It makes him hot.

3. How many petroglyphs are there at this site?

   a. 3 thousand

   b. 6 million

   c. 6 thousand

4. Why is the man excited about a petroglyph of a praying man?

   a. It has a copy on Easter Island.

   b. It's the biggest one.

   c. It shows where to find water.

5. Why is the long "Sky Father" petroglyph so important?

   a. Because it is so hard to see.

   b. Because it has a copy on Easter Island.

   c. Because it is so big.

© CNN

Hawaiian Petroglyph or Rock Carving

6. Some petroglyphs had a practical purpose. For example:

   a. They marked things, such as where to find water.

   b. They showed where a trail was.

   c. Both **a** and **b.**

EXPANDING YOUR LANGUAGE

◇ **Vocabulary Check**

The following words and expressions are useful when reading and writing about places and how they make you feel. You will find these words in the reading selections. You may want to use them in your writing assignment later in the chapter. Check the words you already know. Look up the definitions of new words and add them to your Vocabulary Log.

_____ airy		_____ modern	
_____ bright		_____ noisy	
_____ calm		_____ old-fashioned	
_____ clean		_____ peaceful	
_____ cluttered		_____ shallow	
_____ comfortable		_____ spacious	
_____ crowded		_____ steep	
_____ damp		_____ to be drawn to	
_____ dirty		_____ to feel inspired	
_____ forested		_____ to spend time	
_____ gleaming		_____ uncomfortable	
_____ glow			

◇ **Vocabulary Tip**

Review Antonyms

When you learn a new word, you can expand your vocabulary by reviewing its **antonym,** a word that has the opposite meaning. Review antonyms of the words in the Vocabulary Check. Write the letter of the antonym in the space next to its opposite.

WORDS		ANTONYMS
_e_	1. spacious	a. comfortable
_____	2. modern	b. dry
_____	3. shallow	c. dirty
_____	4. damp	d. old-fashioned
_____	5. clean	e. crowded
_____	6. noisy	f. deep
_____	7. uncomfortable	g. quiet

LANGUAGE LEARNING STRATEGY

Apply the Strategy

Guess the meanings of new words without using a dictionary. Use the **context,** the words around the new word, to help you guess. This will increase your vocabulary and make you a more fluent writer.

First read the following sentences. Guess the meaning of the underlined word in each sentence. Use the other words in the sentences to make your guesses. Then use the Definitions list to check your guesses, and write the letter of the definition next to the correct word.

Sentences

1. The creek is <u>shallow</u> so you can walk across it without getting wet.

2. The path is not <u>steep</u> at all; in fact, it's almost flat.

3. If you take away all the furniture, the room will be very <u>spacious</u>.

4. I'm <u>drawn to</u> that beautiful picture—I look at it whenever I can.

5. I like the <u>forested</u> side of the mountain because the trees give a lot of shade on a hot day.

6. I like to think on long walks in the forest—I <u>feel inspired</u> by the beauty of nature.

Definitions

NEW WORD	MEANING
_b_ 1. shallow	a. not flat
_____ 2. drawn to	b. not deep
_____ 3. spacious	c. attracted to
_____ 4. steep	d. covered with trees
_____ 5. feel inspired	e. having lots of room
_____ 6. forested	f. to have wonderful feelings and ideas

Vocabulary Building

> I went to the woods because I wished to live deliberately, to front only the essential facts of life, and see if I could not learn what it had to teach, and not, when I came to die, discover that I had not lived.
>
> **—HENRY DAVID THOREAU**

Complete the following sentences by giving examples of places you know for the underlined words from the Vocabulary Check.

1. _The school library_ is a <u>spacious</u> place.

2. _____ is a <u>noisy</u> place.

3. _____ is a <u>modern</u> place.

4. _____ is very <u>old-fashioned</u>.

5. I don't like _____ because it's too <u>crowded</u>!

6. _____ is very <u>cluttered</u>.

7. _____ is <u>damp</u>.

8. _____ is <u>clean</u>.

9. _____ is a very <u>peaceful</u> place.

10. I like _____ because it is so <u>comfortable</u>.

Now complete the sentences in this paragraph with the following words from the Vocabulary Check. You might use some more than once.

cluttered	spend time	old-fashioned
damp	uncomfortable	bright
peaceful	calm	

My Favorite Place
·····················

1   My favorite place to work is a room in the basement of my

parents' house. I _____ down there every

day—an hour or so, usually. I go there to do my writing. There

are no windows down there, so it's not very _____.

I have to use a lamp to see my work. It's also very _____

because the walls leak when it rains. And like most basements,

it smells funny.

2   I have a big, _____ desk that my

grandfather gave me. He used it to do his homework when

he was a boy! It's not very neat. In fact, it's completely

_____ with papers, pencils, books, and various

office supplies such as paper clips and staples. My chair is also

very old-fashioned, it's hard and _____,

but I like it anyway.

3   Why do I like this place so much? I _____

down here all alone. Because it's so far from the rest of the

house, and no one ever comes down here, it makes me feel

_____. It's so _____,

I can work for hours.

◈ **Grammar You Can Use:**
Result Clauses:
***so* + adjective (*that*)**

Improve your language skills by using a structure for describing places: *so* + adjective (*that*). You can describe a place by using *so* and an adjective, and a result clause. Look at the examples:

- The beach is *so* <u>cold</u>, you can't go swimming,

- It's *so* <u>quiet</u> on the third floor *that* I can hear myself think!

    so + <u>adjective</u>   (*that*) + result clause

The word *that* at the beginning of the result clause is optional. (You don't *have* to use it.) If you don't use it, combine the two clauses with a comma.

Here are some more examples:

- The cafe is so noisy, it helps me concentrate on my schoolwork.

- I'm up so high, I have a view of the whole city.

- My apartment is so crowded that I can't get any peace and quiet!

LANGUAGE LEARNING STRATEGY

Apply the Strategy

Memorize grammar structures. Then use them as much as you can in your writing. This will help you learn them fast and use them naturally.

Do the following exercise. It will help you remember the new structure: **so + adjective (*that*)**. Then do the next set of exercises. They give you an opportunity to use the structure in writing.

Match the following *so* phrases on the left with the result clauses on the right. (There may be more than one result clause for each *so* phrase.) Write the letter of the result clause next to the *so* + adjective clause it goes with.

_____ 1. The beach is so windy . . .

a. (that) I can't get any work done.

_____ 2. The library is so quiet . . .

b. (that) you can easily get lost.

_____ 3. My dorm room is so noisy . . .

c. (that) you can hear a pin drop.

_____ 4. The city is so big . . .

d. (that) you can't have a conversation.

_____ 5. The woods near my home are so peaceful . . .

e. (that) you can hear yourself think.

First, make up **so + adjective (*that*)** sentences about the following places:

1. my parents' house

2. the cafe in my neighborhood

(continued on next page)

3. the park

4. the school cafeteria

5. the school library

Next, make up five *so* + **adjective** (*that*) sentences about your favorite place. You can write sentences about the place you described in the Freewrite on page 106.

READING FOR WRITING

One of the best ways to improve your writing is to read. Through reading, you can learn about the topic of your writing assignment. You can also study how others write. In this chapter, you will read two selections about places. The first, by Annie Dillard (American, born 1945), is from her book *A Pilgrim at Tinker Creek*. (A *creek* is a small stream.) It describes a favorite place near her Connecticut home. The second is a magazine article about a busy place in a big city in the U.S.

The mountains,
I become a part of it . . .
The morning mists,
the clouds, the gathering waters, I become
a part of it.

—NAVAJO CHANT

◆ **Getting Ready to Read**

Before you read, think about a time when you walked alongside a creek. Discuss the answers to these questions:

- What kinds of plants did you see?

- What kinds of animals did you see?

- What else did you see?
- How did you feel?

As you read, try to answer this question:

- How does the description of Tinker Creek make you *feel*? What words or expressions give you this feeling?

◆Read

Reading 1: A Pilgrim at Tinker Creek

When I slide under the barbed wire fence, cross a field, and run over a sycamore trunk felled[1] across the water, I'm on a little island shaped like a tear in the middle of Tinker Creek. On one side of the creek is a **steep forested** bank; the water is swift and deep on that side of the island. On the other side is the level field I walked through next to the steers'[2] pasture; the water between the field and island is **shallow** and sluggish.[3] In summer's low water, flags and bulrushes[4] grow along a series of **shallow** pools cooled by the lazy current. Water striders[5] patrol the surface film, crayfish[6] hump along the silt bottom eating filth, frogs shout and glare, and shiners and small bream[7] hide among roots from the sulky green heron's[8] eye. I come to this island every month of the year. I walk around it, stopping and staring, or I straddle the sycamore log to read. Today I sit on dry grass at the end of the island by the slower side of the creek. I'm **drawn to** this spot.

—Annie Dillard

◆After You Read

1. What word does Dillard use to describe the shape of the island? Draw a picture of the island.

2. What is the water like on one side of the island? What is it like on the other side?

3. Describe in your own words what the insects, fish, and animals at Tinker Creek are doing.

4. What does Dillard do at Tinker Creek?

[1]**felled:** chopped down; lying down
[2]**steers:** bulls (male cows) used for meat
[3]**sluggish:** slow
[4]**flags, bulrushes:** plants
[5]**water strider:** an insect
[6]**crayfish:** an animal that lives in fresh water; it looks like a small lobster
[7]**shiners and bream:** fish
[8]**heron:** a large wading bird

◆ **Getting Ready to Read**

Before you read, think about a time when you were in a busy train station and answer this question: How did it make you feel? As you read, look for examples of descriptive words and expressions.

◆ **Read**

Reading 2: Grand Central Station

1   Grand Central has changed. You might not recognize this famous train station on 42nd Street in New York City. It's now as **bright** and **clean** as a new coin. There's a statue of Mercury on the south side of the terminal[1]—he's supposed to be the Roman god of business and travel. Now he looks more like Mr. **Clean**, the American god of cleanliness.

Tennessee marble reflects the light from the chandeliers in the Main Concourse of Grand Central Station in New York.

2   Inside, the biggest change is the light. Daylight now pours[2] through four stories[3] of windows on both the east and west sides of the building. **Gleaming** chandeliers,[4] with 144 light bulbs each, add to the natural light. A total of 7500 lights **brighten** the terminal at all hours. Polished Tennessee marble[5] lines[6] the Main Concourse and gives the station a warm **glow**.

3   The old station was dark, **crowded**, and **dirty**. Now it's an **airy** palace of light. There's a holiday mood in the air. You see people move lightly and happily across the Main Concourse. You hear them whistle. You feel **calm**.

◆ **After You Read**

1. What is the main idea of the article? Circle the letter of the sentence that states it best:

   a. Grand Central Station is dark and dirty.

   b. Grand Central Station is the same as it used to be.

   c. Grand Central Station is completely different now.

---

[1]**terminal:** a train station
[2]**pours:** comes in in great amounts
[3]**stories:** floors or levels in a building
[4]**chandelier:** a big light with many light bulbs that hangs from a ceiling
[5]**marble:** a pretty stone that shines when polished
[6]**lines:** covers

2. Compare Grand Central Station in the past with the way it is now. What are some differences?

_____

_____

_____

_____

_____

_____

_____

FROM READING TO WRITING

> **Earth and sky, woods and fields, lakes and rivers, the mountain and the sea, are excellent schoolmasters, and teach some of us more than we can ever learn from books.**
>
> **—SIR JOHN LUBBOCK**

Answer the following questions to prepare for the writing assignment for this chapter. These exercises use the reading selections to teach you about writing.

1. How does the description of Tinker Creek make you feel? Calm? Nervous? Tired? Energetic? Find an adjective that describes your feeling; then list the words and expressions from the excerpt that make you feel this way.

   Adjective: _____

   Examples: _____

   _____

   _____

   _____

2. How does the description of Grand Central Station make you feel? Calm? Nervous? Tired? Energetic? Find an adjective that describes your feeling; then list the words and expressions from the excerpt that make you feel this way.

   Adjective: _____

   Examples: _____

   _____

   _____

   _____

3. Dillard uses a lot of adjectives in her description of Tinker Creek. List them, and say what they describe. Use the following chart.

Adjective	Thing It Describes
shallow	water

4. Dillard includes a lot of details in her description. How many animals does Dillard write about in her description? How many plants does Dillard write about? List them and include words that describe them. Use the following table.

ANIMALS	WHAT THEY LOOK LIKE/ WHAT THEY ARE DOING	PLANTS	WHAT THEY LOOK LIKE/ WHAT THEY ARE DOING
frogs	making noise ("shout")	sycamore trunk	lying across the water

5. Now complete the following table with information about the details in the article about Grand Central Station. What things does the writer tell you about? What do they look like? First list the things. Then write at least one adjective that describes each thing.

THINGS IN GRAND CENTRAL STATION	WHAT THEY LOOK LIKE
chandeliers	gleaming

6. The author of the article about Grand Central Station uses a lot of words that make you think about light. Find these words and list them here:

_____

_____

_____

_____

7. Places often make you feel a certain way. When you describe a place, you say how it makes *you* feel. ("The library is so quiet, it makes me feel *calm*."). You can also say how you feel another way: you can describe things in the place with feeling words. This is what Dillard does. For example, "the water . . . is *sluggish*," "the *lazy* current. . . ."

In this exercise, write about feelings. For each place, say how it makes you feel.

EXAMPLE: library: The library makes me feel calm.

a. my room _____

b. the woods _____

c. the park _____

d. the cafe _____

e. a creek _____

f. a train station _____

Getting Ready to Write

Describing Places

When you describe a place, you show your reader what the place looks like to you. This is just what a painter or a photographer does. However, a writer uses words, expressions, and structures to create the picture of the place. In this chapter, you will practice describing a place using descriptive adjectives and details.

Use Descriptive Adjectives

You can give your reader a clear picture of a place by using descriptive adjectives. You have already learned in this chapter many adjectives that describe places.

Practice To review the adjectives you learned in this chapter, add words that have similar meanings to these words from the Vocabulary Check. Add at least one to each in the list.

calm: _____

crowded: _____

gleaming: _____

modern: _____

spacious: _____

Include Details

Another way to describe a place is to give a lot of details, such as things, animals, or people you find at the place. You can describe them with adjectives, and/or you can say what they are doing.

Practice Think about the things, animals, or people you might see in each of these places. Write your ideas in the blanks.

a forest: _____

_____

_____

_____

a train station: _____

_____

_____

_____

a park: _____

_____

_____

_____

Choose a Topic

You will write a description of a place that creates one of the following feelings. Use the following list to help you decide on a place to describe:

- nervous
- happy

- calm
- creative

- energetic
- uncomfortable

Plan Your Writing

Even if the place you chose to describe is one where you spend a lot of time every day, go at least one more time and really *look* at it. Take notes on this place. Write down notes on the following:

1. What does it look like?

2. What things, animals, or people do you find there?

3. What are they doing?

4. What do you do in this place?

5. How does the place make you feel?

Study an Example

Read this example of a student essay and answer the questions that follow.

My Favorite Place

1   My favorite place when I was a child was the attic in my parents' house. To an eight-year-old kid like I was, the attic appeared really huge and the stairs enormously tall. Every time I climbed those big wooden steps, it was an adventure. Once I got there, it was heaven. The attic wasn't very organized; as a matter of fact, it wasn't organized at all. But that was the beauty of it. I could play with anything that I chose and didn't have to put it back the way it was. Nobody could tell the difference.

2   The attic was composed of many unusual and interesting objects. A few of my favorites were my dad's fishing poles, a miniature-sized chalk board, a broken classical guitar, and my most favorite of all, my mom's old clothes and her costume jewelry. I would pretend that I was fishing in a pond, telling my dad to lower his voice so he wouldn't scare the fish away. I would play the role of my dad and myself, conversing back and forth. When playing fishing bored me after awhile, I banged on the old guitar that was hanging by the entrance. But I could never make a good sound, so I quit plucking on the strings, not that I was a bad player, but because the guitar

> There is a pleasure in
>   the pathless woods,
> There is a rapture on
>   the lonely shore,
> There is society,
>   where none intrudes.
> By the deep sea, and
>   music in its roars;
> I love not man the less,
>   but nature more.
>
> **—GEORGE GORDON BYRON**

was old and broken. After abusing the guitar, I would write on the chalkboard, pretending to be a teacher, scribbling words that I didn't even know and erasing them and scribbling them again. It was fun. I saved the best for last: playing with my mom's old clothes and jewelry. I would put on her old lingerie and pretend to be a princess, telling my imaginary servants to bring me snacks. My mom had so many old outfits, I kept changing until I got bored to death. I mixed a pink blouse with a floral skirt, a floral skirt with a tank top, a tank top with bell-bottom pants, and so on. It was the best thing a little girl could do; it was fun.

—Joo Hee Cho

1. Did the writer choose an interesting topic?

2. Did she give you a clear picture of the place she was describing? Did she include a lot of details? Did she use descriptive adjectives?

3. What did you like about the student example?

4. Do you have any advice or suggestions for Joo Hee?

Write

Write a description of a place that creates one of the feelings in Choose Your Topic. Describe how the place looks. Use lots of descriptive adjectives. Include important things, animals, or people you find there, what you do there, and how the place makes you feel. Use at least one result clause (*so* + adjective [*that*]).

After You Write

Revise

After you write a draft of your essay, have someone else read it and give you suggestions on how to improve it. Exchange your paper with a classmate or give your paper to your teacher, your mentor, or a friend to evaluate by answering these questions:

Questions for Revision	Yes	No
1. Does the writer use lots of descriptive adjectives? Notes:		
2. Does the writer talk about things, people, or animals in the place? Notes:		

Questions for Revision	Yes	No
3. Does the writer describe how the place makes him or her feel? Notes:		
4. Are there any comments or recommendations you can make to improve this paper? If yes, write here something the writer could do:		

Plan your revision by reading the evaluation. Talk with your teacher or classmates about what you can do to improve this essay. Write some notes in case you choose to rewrite this paper later.

Edit

Now review your writing for correctness. Look at spelling, punctuation, and grammar. Read and respond to this checklist alone; then exchange papers and ask a classmate to answer these questions:

Questions for Editing	Yes	No
1. Does the writer use vocabulary that is specific and correct? Notes:		
2. Does the writer use at least one result clause (*so* + adjective [*that*])? Notes:		
3. Are there any grammar mistakes you want to point out? If yes, what should the writer check?		

Correct any mistakes your classmate or teacher pointed out in the Editing Checklist. Now you are ready to place your writing in your

Writing Portfolio. You may choose to rewrite it or expand it to a longer piece now or later.

PUTTING IT ALL TOGETHER

Use What You Have Learned

Write about another place. Refer to your teacher's or classmate's feedback on your writing from this chapter to write quickly and effectively. Read your writing to the class.

Test-Taking Tip

Before you begin writing, decide how you will divide your time. If you are taking a test which asks you to answer six essay questions, all with the same point value, you should split your time equally between each question. If you are still working on a question at the end of the time you have allowed for that question, stop writing, leave space, and begin the next question. If you have time at the end of the test, you can go back to finish any incomplete answers.

CHECK YOUR PROGRESS

On a scale of 1 to 5, rate how well you have mastered the goals set at the beginning of the chapter:

1 2 3 4 5   use descriptive adjectives and details to describe a place.

1 2 3 4 5   use a journal to connect your personal life to school assignments.

1 2 3 4 5   guess the meanings of new words in context.

1 2 3 4 5   use result clauses: *so* + adjective (*that*).

1 2 3 4 5   memorize grammar structures.

If you've given yourself a 3 or lower on any of these goals:

- visit the *Tapestry* web site for additional practice.
- ask your instructor for extra help.
- review the sections of the chapter that you found difficult.
- work with a partner or study group to further your progress.

"When they say that music is a universal language, it really is true. Through music, we are able to connect with other people and to understand just how valuable the human community is."

—Paul Simon

Read the quotation by Paul Simon. What does he think about music? Do you agree with him? Write down something you've learned from listening to music from a different country than your own:

_____

_____

_____

_____

MUSICAL AMBASSADORS

World musicians are international messengers. Their music helps us understand that people throughout the world share many of the same feelings. Their music also teaches us about differences: differences in musical traditions, musical styles, and musical instruments. In this chapter, you will talk and read about world musicians. Then you will write about a musician who interests you.

Setting Goals

In this chapter, you will practice writing to inform. Specifically, you will write about a world musician. You will choose and organize information and add your opinion. In order to do this, you will:

◈ listen to music to improve your English.

◈ group new words into categories.

◈ learn to combine sentences by using *not only . . . , but also*.

◈ use the television as a learning tool.

What additional goals do you have for this chapter? Write them here:

_____

_____

◇ Getting Started

With a partner, brainstorm a list of world musicians you know. A world musician can be someone who:

- is well-known in most parts of the world or
- plays music from many different countries and/or cultures or
- plays and/or performs with other international musicians or
- sings in more than one language or
- is a combination of these.

Write down the names of all the world musicians you can think of:

_____   _____   _____   _____

_____   _____   _____   _____

_____   _____   _____   _____

MEETING THE TOPIC

• •

A.   B.   C.   D.   E.   F.

Look at the photos of musicians from the past and present. How many of them do you recognize? Work with a partner to match names with photos.

_____ Bob Marley   _____ Yanni

_____ Luis Miguel   _____ U2

_____ Celine Dion   _____ Miriam Makeba

Give and get information about the musicians in the photos. Work with at least four different classmates, one at a time, to complete as much of the chart as possible.

Name of Musician/ Group	Where from/ Language They Use	When and Where Popular	Type of Music/Musical Instrument(s)	Names of Songs	Opinions About Musician

LANGUAGE LEARNING STRATEGY

Apply the Strategy

Listen to music to improve your English. Music can be a powerful tool for increasing your language learning. Listening to music can help you increase your fluency and understand the culture.

Listen to some popular music. If possible, choose a selection from one of the world musicians you've discussed. Listen to the words of the songs. Write down the important words and phrases. Think about what they mean. Bring the music to class and share it with your classmates.

 Freewrite

You've had a chance to look, listen, and talk. Here is your first opportunity to write about a musician of your choice. Write as quickly as you can. You may choose to use this writing (or some of the ideas) for the writing assignment later in the chapter.

TUNING IN: "Angelique Kidjo"

The CNN video you will watch is an interview with Angelique Kidjo, a singer from West Africa. Later in this chapter you will read

© CNN

**Angelique Kidjo
in performance**

about her. Read the following questions first. Then watch the video and answer the questions.

1. How many languages does Angelique speak?

   a. 2

   b. 4

   c. 8

2. What does Angelique believe about how language is used in music?

   a. You must understand English to understand her music.

   b. The emotion of a song is more important than the language.

   c. Singers should speak many languages.

3. What helped Angelique become a musician?

   a. Her family was very musical.

   b. She listened to many other musicians from around the world.

   c. Both of these.

4. What kind of music does Angelique perform?

   a. pop rock

   b. melting pot

   c. jazz

5. What is Angelique's "first love"?

   a. recording

   b. listening to other musicians

   c. performing

EXPANDING YOUR LANGUAGE

Vocabulary Check

The following words and expressions are useful when reading and writing about world musicians and international music. You will find these words in the reading selections. You may want to use them in your writing assignment later in the chapter. Check the words you already know. Look up the definitions of new words and add them to your Vocabulary Log.

> I've always thought musicians would be great politicians and are great ambassadors.
>
> **—ONE MUSICIAN REFLECTING ON A SAXOPHONE PERFORMANCE BY U.S. PRESIDENT BILL CLINTON**

_____ bass	_____ lyrics	_____ salsa
_____ chorus	_____ orchestra	_____ samba
_____ composer	_____ polyglot	_____ showman
_____ energetic	_____ pop	_____ soul
_____ funk	_____ powerful	_____ spectacular
_____ gospel	_____ reggae	_____ synthesizer
_____ influences	_____ rhythm	_____ talented
_____ jazz	_____ rock and roll	_____ unique
_____ keyboard	_____ rumba	_____ unusual

◇**Vocabulary Tip**

Use the Suffix -_ist_ to Describe Musical Performers

Add to your vocabulary by changing some words you already know. By adding the suffix -_ist_ to the name of certain musical instruments, you have the name of the person who plays that instrument. For example, a musician who plays the _guitar_ is a _guitarist_. Practice forming names for musicians who play these instruments by adding -_ist_ as an ending.

guitar _guitarist_

piano* _____ bass _____

flute* _____ violin _____

percussion _____ saxophone* _____

vocal _____ (This musician "plays her voice" or is a singer.)

lyric _____ (This person writes words for music.)

*Drop the final letter before adding the suffix in these words.

LANGUAGE LEARNING STRATEGY

Group new words and ideas into categories. Grouping words into categories where their meanings or use are related will help you learn and remember the words more easily.

(continued on next page)

Apply the Strategy

Put as many words as you can from the Vocabulary Check into groups of similar meanings. Give each category a name. The same word can appear in more than one group. Start with these groups and make more groups if you can. Add some words of your own. Share your word groups with the class.

Group 1: Words That Describe Music

Group 2: Words That Describe Musicians

Group 3: Instruments

Group 4: Dance Styles

◇ Vocabulary Building

Check the meanings of these words by circling the letter of the correct answer.

1. A *composer*

   a. writes music or creates musical selections.

   b. writes lyrics.

   c. writes books about music.

2. A *keyboard* is not a

   a. piano.

   b. synthesizer.

   c. guitar.

3. A *polyglot* musician

   a. plays several instruments.

   b. speaks several languages.

   c. knows many other musicians.

4. Members of a *chorus*

   a. dance.

   b. play drums.

   c. sing.

5. A *talented* saxophonist

   a. plays the saxophone well.

   b. doesn't play the saxophone well.

   c. wants to learn the saxophone.

Complete the following paragraph by selecting one of the words in the box.

rhythms	lyrics	guitarist	unique	pop	unusual

American-Based African Musicians

More and more musicians from Africa are living in the U.S. American-based African musicians practice their musical traditions and learn new styles at the same time. One of the most interesting African musicians living in the U.S. is Samba Ngo, who comes from the central African country of Congo (see map on page 135). Ngo, who lives

both in California and North Carolina, is a singer and a (1) _____. He also plays the *likembe*, an African thumb piano. His music is a (2) _____ form of African (3) _____. It combines traditional and modern instruments as well as traditional and modern musical styles. It has lots of beats and mixes a variety of (4) _____. The (5) _____ in Samba's songs are also (6) _____. He sings in Lingala, Kikongo, Mounukutouba, French, and English about politics, relationships, and history. Samba believes that music is medicine, no matter what country it comes from.

Grammar You Can Use: Sentence Combining with *not only . . . , but also*

You can combine facts into one sentence by using the structure *not only . . . , but also*. Look at the example:

> *Not only* does he sing beautifully, *but* he is *also* an excellent guitarist.

In the example, the writer has combined these two facts:

> He sings beautifully. He is an excellent guitarist.

Notice that the subject and verb (or auxilliary) are inverted (they change order). There is a comma between the two parts of the sentence.

Practice using the structure by combining these sentences:

1. She speaks five languages. She plays three musical instruments.

   _____

   _____

   _____

> **If music could change the world, the world would already be free.**
>
> **—HUGH MASAKELA**

2. Mampouya is a master drummer. He plays the *likembe*.

   _____

   _____

   _____

3. Paul Simon played folk music in the sixties. He plays world music now.

   _____

   _____

   _____

READING FOR WRITING

One of the best ways to improve your writing is to read. Through reading, you can learn about the topic of your writing assignment. You can also study how others write. In this chapter, you will read two selections about world musicians. The first selection is from a newspaper article about Yanni, a musician who lives in North America but is originally from Greece. The second selection is from a web site about Angelique Kidjo, the singer from Africa you saw in Tuning In.

◆**Getting Ready to Read**

Before you read, discuss your answers to these questions:

- Have you heard of Yanni or listened to his music?
- Yanni likes to have concerts in huge, spectacular locations around the world. What places could Yanni choose for his concerts?

◆**Read**

Reading 1: Yanni

1 Yanni, a **composer** and **keyboard** player originally from Greece, plays what is sometimes called easy-listening music. He is one of the biggest stars from the New Age movement of the eighties. His music reflects his kindness, his energy, and his sentimental nature. It is music looking for a movie.

2 Yanni's shows are always **spectacular.** The lights, close-up video display, and smoke machines make the tiny man look bigger than he is. He has long, thick black hair, wears all white, and has a toothpaste-commercial smile. He is an **energetic showman** on stage, jumping up from the piano and skipping across the stage to the **synthesizers** several times during a show, shaking his hair from front to back and flashing his broad smile.

3 The very successful musician chooses concert locations that are also spectacular. He and his large group of accompanying musicians have performed at the Acropolis, the Taj Mahal, and the Forbidden City. His songs include traditional instruments from all over the world: the Chinese flute, Armenian horn, and Aborigine digeridoo. The combination of instruments and multicultural music (**rock** rhythms, Spanish guitar sounds, Mediterranean melodies like "Zorba the Greek") make Yanni a musical cook of **polyglot** international stew. All he needs is a white chef's hat to complete his costume.

◆**After You Read**

1. Which sentences are true for Yanni?

   a. He combines different kinds of instruments.

   b. He combines different kinds of music.

   c. Both of these.

2. What do you think these expressions mean?

    a. Yanni's music "is music looking for a movie."

    _____

    _____

    _____

    b. Yanni has a "toothpaste-commercial smile."

    _____

    _____

    _____

    c. Yanni is "a musical cook of polyglot international stew."

    _____

    _____

    _____

3. What did you find interesting or surprising about Yanni?

    _____

    _____

    _____

◇**Getting Ready to Read**

Before you read, answer this question: What can you predict about Angelique or her music knowing that she comes from Africa? As you read, look for the one general idea that makes Angelique unique.

◇**Read**

Reading 2: Angelique Kidjo

1   Angelique Kidjo is one of Africa's most **powerful** and engaging young female stars. Her music uses **rhythms** from the music of her native country, Benin, and adds **reggae, samba, funk,** and **gospel** to create a **unique** sound.

2   Kidjo was born in Benin, West Africa. She comes from a musical family and has eight brothers and sisters. Her mother is a dance and theater director, and her brother is a guitarist.

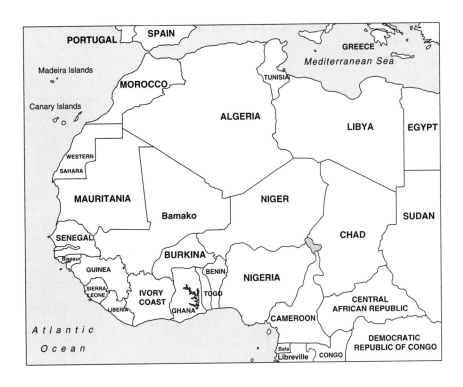

Angelique listened to traditional West African music when she was growing up. She also listened to **salsa, rumba** from the Congo, makossa from Cameroon, **soul,** funk, and even Arabic and Indian music. Kidjo brought all these different styles into her own music. She sings many songs in her native language, Fon,* but she also sings in French, English, Yoruba,* and Ewe.*

3   Early in her career, Kidjo traveled from Benin to France, where she met talented musicians from Africa, the Caribbean, France, and North America. She studied **jazz** in Paris and developed her own musical style. This is how she describes her music: "Some call it Afro-funk. You can call it whatever you like, but really, it's hard to put my music into one category. Even when I use traditional music, I don't play just one style, I mix it all up."

4   *Fifa,* one of Kidjo's recent albums, is an **unusual** mix of modern and ancient music. Many of the songs use traditional drum rhythms, which Kidjo and her husband, a French composer and **bass** player, recorded during a visit to villages in Benin. The first line of one song is: "I've been away for so long that I wonder if the sound of the drums still has its power." Kidjo explains: "I wanted

*Fon, Yoruba, and Ewe are West African languages.

to go back to my country. I really missed those drums." If you listen to the music, you will hear the power of the drums.

5   *Oremi,* the most recent album, also brings together different languages and musical styles. There are South African Xhosa **choruses,** jazz rhythms, English, and Fon. Is Kidjo worried because listeners may not understand the words of her songs? "I don't feel concerned," she says. "Music is a language that everyone understands." Kidjo believes that if people don't understand her music through its **lyrics,** they will understand it through the feelings it expresses.

◆After You Read

> **Music is the only thing that can bring us together.**
>
> **—ANGELIQUE KIDJO**

1. What influenced Angelique to become a musician?

   _____

   _____

   _____

2. What does Angelique's music mix?

   _____

   _____

   _____

3. What did Angelique and her husband do when they visited Benin?

   _____

   _____

   _____

4. Does Angelique believe that listeners have to understand her lyrics to enjoy her music? Do you agree with her?

   _____

   _____

   _____

FROM READING TO WRITING

Answer the following questions to prepare for the writing assignment in this chapter. These exercises use the reading selections to teach you about writing.

1. Which kinds of information did you see in the readings about Yanni and Angelique Kidjo? Put a check next to the facts you found for each of the musicians.

   Yanni   Angelique

   _____   _____   The names of his/her most popular songs

   _____   _____   Where and how he/she learned to compose

   _____   _____   What he/she looks like

   _____   _____   Where he/she has performed

   _____   _____   People he/she has dedicated his/her songs to

   _____   _____   Which instrument(s) he/she plays

   _____   _____   Musical styles

   Did either of the reading selections include *all* of these different kinds of information?

   Yes   No

2. Each of the paragraphs in "Angelique Kidjo" is developed around a topic. The topics are listed below, but not in the order they appear. Reorder them according to how they appear in the reading.

   _____ Her most recent album includes different languages and musical styles.

   _____ She is a great modern singer who mixes many musical styles.

   _____ One of her albums combines modern and traditional music.

   _____ Her background includes many musical influences.

   _____ Much of her training took place in France with well-known musicians.

3. Most of the sentences in the two selections are facts. Do you see sentences that express an opinion? Where are they? Write them here.

   _____

   _____

   _____

   _____

◆**Getting Ready to Write**

Writing About a World Musician

When you write about a world musician, there are a few things you can do to make your writing clear and interesting. You should limit and organize your information and present your opinion. Follow these tips.

Limit Your Information

There are many different kinds of information a writer can include when writing to inform. Look at the chart below, which includes some different kinds of information you can include when describing a world musician.

• musician's childhood and family background	• musical education	• instrument(s) or type(s) of music musician plays or sings
• languages musician speaks and sings in	• musical style/types of music	• who/what influenced musician
• most popular songs	• highlights of musician's career	• what inspires musician/musician's feelings or beliefs

When writing about a world musician, don't try to include all these facts. Don't write everything you know about the subject. Choose two or three different important facts. Make your writing clear by limiting the information you include. The information you choose should show how the musician is unique.

Practice You will begin to write about a world musician of your choice in the next section. Circle two or three kinds of information in the chart above that you would like to include in your writing.

Organize Your Ideas in Paragraphs

Make your writing easy to understand by developing paragraphs around related ideas. The sentences in one paragraph should all be related to the topic of that paragraph. For example, if you are writing one paragraph about a musician's background, don't include a sentence about the musician's future plans.

Practice Choose one paragraph from either of the reading selections. What is the topic of the paragraph? Give the paragraph a title and share it with your classmates.

Include Your Opinion or a Personal Experience

Sometimes writing about a world musician is more interesting if you include your opinion about that person or if you describe a personal experience. Ask your teacher if this is permitted on the assignment for this chapter. (Sometimes teachers do not want the writer's opinions in informative writing.) Sentences including your opinion can come at the beginning or end of your essay.

Practice Write at least one sentence that includes your opinion about a world musician. Be sure to include the reason(s) for your opinion.

Choose a Topic

Now decide the topic of your essay for this chapter. Use the list below to help you choose. Write about:

- a world musician you like
- a world musician you either know a lot about or want to learn more about
- two musicians who come from the same region/country/culture/ language background
- two musicians who faced similar challenges
- two musicians who are extremely popular

Plan Your Writing

Gather information about the musician or musicians you selected. The following activities will help you.

1. Do several of these activities and write down the information you collect:

   - listen to some music by the musician(s) you selected.
   - watch a TV program about the music or musician(s) you selected.
   - watch a music video of the musician(s) you selected.
   - talk to some friends about the musician(s) you selected.
   - read some cassette covers or CD liners of the musician(s) you selected.

- read a newspaper or magazine review of the musician(s) you selected.

- interview a musician or someone who works at a music store about the musician(s) you selected.

ACADEMIC POWER STRATEGY

Apply the Strategy

Use the television as a learning tool. Although many TV programs aren't educational, there are some that are. Watching these programs can help you learn English quickly, teach you about different cultures, and help you with school assignments.

Gather information about a world musician by watching television. First, study a TV schedule to find a program on a world musician. Perhaps there is one channel that presents music all the time. Watch at least one television program and take notes in the chart below. Report to your class on what you learned.

TELEVISION AS TEACHER: WORLD MUSICIANS				
Channel	Time	Name of Program	Musician Featured	What I Learned
Vocabulary and Expressions I Learned:				

2. Choose the information you want to include in your writing about a musician. Organize it around one to three topics. If you are going to include your opinion, think about where you will put it. Use the diagram below to organize your ideas:

Introduction and General Idea About Musician(s) That Tells Why He or She Is Unique
(You may present your opinion or explain why you chose this musician.)

Possible Topic 1: Early Years, Important Influences

Possible Topic 2: Training, Lucky Opportunities, Successful Events

Possible Topic 3: Current Information—Recent Concerts, Albums, Interests

Possible Topic 4: Musician's Future Plans, Hopes

Conclusion

Study an Example

Read this essay written by a student and answer the questions that follow.

Be Happy: Bobby McFerrin's Performing

1   Bobby McFerrin is a multi-talented American musician. He sings and conducts music from a variety of historical periods and musical traditions. As a young boy in New York, he listened to the gospel music of his parents' church. In these early years, he learned that music can entertain, heal, bring people together, and inspire.

2   McFerrin became famous with his playful popular song "Don't Worry, Be Happy," but his talent extends far beyond singing simple melodies. In fact, his voice is an amazing musical instrument. He can sing like a violin, a drum, or a piano. He can sing high and soft

or low and heavy. He imitates perfectly a wide variety of musical instruments as well as insects and animals.

3   Not only does he sing a range of styles and sounds, but he also conducts classical orchestras. He is currently director of the Saint Paul Chamber Orchestra. He has made recordings with world musicians such as Yo-Yo Ma and Chick Corea. He has performed with Voicestra, a group of twelve singers who create songs as they sing them.

4   McFerrin's music is always fresh and original. His many talents continue to surprise and delight audiences and show the many different sounds and feelings music can produce. Like his early popular song suggests, don't worry when Bobby's performing!

> **Music is potentially one of the greatest healing forces we have.**
>
> **—BOBBY MCFERRIN**

1. What are two facts you learned about Bobby McFerrin?

     a. _____

     b. _____

2. What does the writer like about this musician?

     _____

     _____

3. What did you notice or like about this example?

     _____

     _____

4. What question or suggestion do you have for this writer?

     _____

     _____

◇ **Write**

Now write about a world musician. Review what you learned in this chapter. You may use the writing you've already begun. Remember to limit and organize your information and show how the musician is unique.

◇ **After You Write**

Revise

After writing a draft of your essay, have someone else read it and give you suggestions on how to improve it. Exchange your paper with a classmate or give your paper to your teacher or another reader and ask them to evaluate it by answering these questions:

Questions for Revision	Yes	No
1. Has the writer limited the information to support one general idea about why the musician is unique or unusual? Notes:		
2. Has the writer organized the information in paragraphs around different topics that support the main idea? Notes:		
3. Is there any information about the musician that does **not** support or relate to the main idea or supporting topics? Notes:		
4. Would you like to know something else about the musician? If yes, suggest something the writer should add:		

Plan your revision by reading the evaluation. Talk with your teacher or classmates about what you can do to improve this essay. Write some notes in case you choose to rewrite this paper later.

Edit

Now review your writing for correctness. Look at spelling, punctuation, and grammar. Read and respond to this checklist alone; then exchange papers and ask a classmate to answer these questions:

Questions for Editing	Yes	No
1. Does the writer use vocabulary that is specific and correct? Notes:		
2. Is the expression *not only . . . but also* used correctly? Notes:		
3. Are there any grammar mistakes you want to point out? If yes, write what the writer should check:		

Correct any mistakes your classmate or teacher pointed out in the Editing Checklist. Now you are ready to place your writing in your Writing Portfolio. You may choose to rewrite it or expand it to a longer piece now or later.

PUTTING IT ALL TOGETHER

◇ **Use What You Have Learned**

Go to a world music concert and write about the musician(s). Refer to your teacher's or classmate's feedback on your writing from this chapter to write quickly and effectively. Read your writing to the class.

Test-Taking Tip

Keep your focus on the test. Don't worry about your ability, the behavior of other students, the number of questions, or anything else. Pay close attention to one question at a time. This kind of concentration focuses your thinking and reduces anxiety. If you are too nervous to think or read carefully, try to slow down physically by taking several slow, deep breaths. Then start to work.

CHECK YOUR PROGRESS

On a scale of 1 to 5, rate how well you have mastered the goals set at the beginning of the chapter:

1 2 3 4 5   choose and organize information to write about a world musician.

1 2 3 4 5   listen to music to improve your English.

1 2 3 4 5   group new words into categories.

1 2 3 4 5   combine sentences by using *not only . . . , but also.*

1 2 3 4 5   use the television as a learning tool.

If you've given yourself a 3 or lower on any of these goals:

- visit the *Tapestry* web site for additional practice.
- ask your instructor for extra help.
- review the sections of the chapter that you found difficult.
- work with a partner or study group to further your progress.

"We eat whenever life becomes dramatic: at weddings, birthdays, funerals, at parting and at welcoming home, or at any moment which a group decides is worthy of remark."

—Margaret Visser

R ead the quotation by Margaret Visser about eating for special occasions. What do you think she means? Do you agree? Write about a celebration when you remember the food:

_____

_____

_____

_____

7

LET'S PARTY!

Celebrations are important moments in our lives such as birthdays, weddings, and holidays. Thinking about these important events can help us understand others and ourselves better. In this chapter, you are going to talk and write about your favorite celebration and explain its meaning and purpose.

Setting Goals

In this chapter, you will practice describing an event. Specifically, you will describe a celebration. You will organize paragraphs around main ideas and use descriptive adjectives about celebrations. In order to do this, you will:

◈ review the use of separable and inseparable phrasal verbs.

◈ look for words and expressions in reading passages that you can use in your own writing.

◈ study how other writers organize ideas.

◈ study with a partner.

What additional goals do you have for this chapter? Write them here:

_____

_____

147

◆**Getting Started**

Think about your favorite celebration. Now work with a partner. Ask your partner about his or her favorite celebration. It can be a holiday, a birthday, a wedding, or another celebration. Start with the following questions, and then add some of your own:

1. What's your favorite celebration? Why is it your favorite?

2. What is the purpose of this celebration?

3. What do you usually do for this celebration?

4. Do you prepare any special foods for this celebration?

5. Do your wear special clothes?

6. Are there any special decorations?

7. Your questions:

_____

_____

_____

MEETING THE TOPIC

Look at the photos of celebrations in different countries. For each photo, answer these questions: What is happening? Where is it happening? What is the name of the celebration? Work with a partner.

A. _____

_____

B. _____

_____

C. _____

_____

D. _____

_____

E. _____

_____

F. _____

_____

Give and get information about the celebrations in the photos. Use the following questions. For each piece of information that you get from a classmate, give a new fact. After you exchange information, move on to a new classmate. Try to fill in as much of the following chart as you can.

1. What is the name of the celebration?

2. What is the reason for this celebration?

3. What do people do (activities) during this celebration?

4. What do people eat for this celebration?

5. What do people wear for this celebration?

6. Are there special decorations for this celebration? What are they?

	Name	Reason	Special Activities	Special Food	Special Clothing	Special Decorations	Other Facts
A.							
B.							
C.							
D.							
E.							
F.							

Freewrite

> **Celebrations are the juice of life.**
>
> —JOHN D. HOFBRAUER, JR.

You've had a chance to look, listen, and talk. Now connect your ideas in writing. Write about a celebration. Write about why people celebrate it, and the special foods, activities, clothes, and decorations associated with it. You can write notes or sentences or make a list. Write as quickly as you can. Don't worry about grammar or spelling; just get your ideas on paper.

TUNING IN: "Costumes at Carnival"

© CNN

Costumes at Carnival in Venice

The CNN video you will watch is about Carnival in Venice, Italy. Read the following questions first. Then watch the video and answer the questions.

1. When does Carnival take place in Venice?

   a. in January

   b. in February

   c. in March

2. How many days does Carnival last?

   a. twelve

   b. ten

   c. seven

3. How does the announcer describe the Venetian Carnival?

   a. It's one of the world's longest.

   b. It's one of the world's most colorful.

   c. It's one of the world's biggest.

4. What does the Venice Carnival parade celebrate?

   a. The city.

   b. Some of the city's most famous characters.

   c. Both **a** and **b.**

5. How does the announcer describe the nighttime costumes at Carnival?

   a. They're a little lighter.

   b. They're a little louder.

   c. They're a little brighter.

EXPANDING YOUR LANGUAGE

Vocabulary Check   The following words and expressions are useful when reading and writing about celebrations. You will find these words in the reading selections. You may want to use them in your writing assignment later in the chapter. Check the words you already know. Look up the definitions of new words and add them to your Vocabulary Log.

_____ abundance	_____ symbol
_____ banquet	_____ to be based on
_____ buffet	_____ to bring luck
_____ carnival	_____ to celebrate
_____ celebration	_____ to dress up
_____ dragon	_____ to emphasize
_____ dumpling	_____ to ensure
_____ evil spirit	_____ to mark
_____ feast	_____ to mean
_____ fireworks	_____ to play tricks
_____ longevity	_____ to scare away
_____ open house	_____ to signify
_____ pastry	_____ to symbolize
_____ prosperity	_____ traditional
_____ rite of passage	

Vocabulary Tip   **Put Words into Categories**

You can increase your vocabulary and remember new words more easily if you group them into categories. Find words in the Vocabulary Check that fit into the following categories. Write them on the lines.

Words that describe special meals:

_____

_____

_____

Words that describe foods:

_____

_____

Words that describe good things you wish for in life:

_____

_____

◆ Vocabulary Building

Complete the sentences in the following paragraph by selecting one of the words in the box. You may use a word more than one time.

feasts	celebrate	signifies
symbolizes	ensure	scare away

Kwanzaa is an African-American holiday held December 26th through January 1st. The seven-day celebration encourages African-Americans to think about their African roots as well as their life in present day America. Kwanzaa, which was started in 1966, is based on African festivals. The word means "the first fruits."

Chinese New Year

Chinese New Year is my favorite celebration. It's a special time. It _____ that spring has begun. For Chinese New Year, we do many special things. One thing we do is clean our houses from top to bottom. A clean house _____ a new beginning. Another thing we do to _____ the new year is get our hair cut and wear new clothes. Also, families get together for big _____. Each dish we eat _____ something. For example, we always have a big roasted chicken to _____ wealth in the coming year. We also have a dragon parade and fireworks in the street. The dragon and fireworks _____ evil spirits and _____ that everyone will have a happy new year.

Grammar You Can Use: Phrasal Verbs

Some of the verbs in the Vocabulary Check are **phrasal verbs.** Phrasal verbs are verbs followed by an adverb or a preposition.

EXAMPLE: scare away

We light fireworks to *scare away* evil spirits.

An object can separate some phrasal verbs, but some cannot be separated.

EXAMPLES:

We light fireworks to *scare* evil spirits *away.* (separable)

When dinner starts, everyone *sits down* at the table. (inseparable)

Study this chart of separable and inseparable phrasal verbs and their meanings.

Separable	Meaning	Inseparable	Meaning
scare away	frighten	sit down	sit
dress up	put on special clothes	drop by	visit
pick up	buy or get	go to	attend
clean up	clean	stay up	stay awake
open up	open	grow up	become an adult
let go	release		
put up	place		

Complete the following sentences with phrasal verbs from the chart.

1. For Halloween, we always _____ in scary costumes.

2. It's a custom to _____ the house _____ just before New Year's.

3. When we lived in England, friends and family used to _____ _____ our house for food on Boxing Day, December 26.

4. I like to _____ late on Christmas Eve.

5. Some people _____ restaurants for Thanksgiving dinner.

6. The purpose of the dancing dragon in the Chinese New Year Parade

   is to _____ evil spirits _____.

Now rewrite your freewrite using three phrasal verbs.

READING FOR WRITING

One of the best ways to improve your writing is to read. Through reading, you can learn about the topic of your writing assignment. You can also study how others write. In this chapter, you will read two selections about celebrations. The first is an interview. Five people answered this question: What is your favorite celebration? The second is a newspaper article about a New Year celebration.

Getting Ready to Read

The people in the interview do not say the name of their favorite celebration. As you read each answer, try to answer these questions:

* What is the name of this celebration?

* Where (in what part of the world) does it take place?

Read

Reading 1: What Is Your Favorite Celebration?

a. This is my favorite **celebration** because we get to **dress up** in scary costumes. Sometimes we have a parade at school in our costumes. Then, at night, when it gets dark, we go to our neighbors' houses in our  costumes. When people answer the door, we shout "Trick or treat!" Then they give us candy. We always get candy, and we never **play tricks** on anybody.

b. This was the happiest day of my life. We had the **celebration** at my parents' home. We put strings of colored lights up around the house so everyone would know that a special event was taking place. All of my nieces and nephews led a parade to my house. They carried candles. After the ceremony, we had a wonderful **feast.** There was music and belly dancing for entertainment.

c. Girls in my country have this **celebration** when they are fifteen years old. It's a **rite of passage**—a **celebration** that tells everyone that a change has happened. This **rite of passage** says: On this day, a girl becomes an adult. The girl wears a fancy pink dress. All the other girls wear pretty, pastel [light-colored] dresses. The boys wear suits. We are very grown up on this day! We go to church. Then we have a dinner-dance. The girl has the first dance with her father; then she dances with her boyfriend. That **symbolizes** the family letting go of the girl. After we dance, we have cake and open presents.

d. This **celebration** is in February. It is a religious **celebration.** This **celebration** signifies the last chance to have fun before the long, serious period before Easter. We wear costumes and masks in the streets. We eat a special food at this time, too—a fried **pastry** sprinkled with sugar. There are many cultural events, such as concerts and plays. But the biggest event is a ball [a dance] in St. Mark's Square. People stay up all night dancing in the streets in their wonderful costumes.

e. This is my favorite **celebration**! Last year, I invited six girls to my party. We played games, and the winners got prizes. Then I opened my presents. I got some jewelry, some paints, and some doll clothes. After the presents, we had cake and ice cream, and everyone sang to me!

The first American Thanksgiving was celebrated in 1621, the year after the Pilgrims arrived on Plymouth Rock. The Thanksgiving meal celebrated the Pilgrims' first harvest in America. In 1863 President Abraham Lincoln made Thanksgiving an official annual holiday. It is now celebrated on the 4th Thursday of November each year. The Thanksgiving meal usually includes a stuffed turkey, yams, potatoes, corn, and cranberry sauce. It is traditional for relatives to gather together to share this meal.

LANGUAGE LEARNING STRATEGY

Apply the Strategy

When you read, look for words and expressions that you can use in your writing. Circle them or write them in your Vocabulary Log, and study them so you can use them later when you write.

Reread the descriptions of celebrations on page 154 and 155. Find words and expressions that you think you can use in your writing assignment for this chapter. Circle them or write them in your Vocabulary Log.

◆ **After You Read**

1. Work in small groups. First, guess the names of each celebration in "What Is Your Favorite Celebration?" Write your guesses here:

   a. _____   d. _____

   b. _____   e. _____

   c. _____

2. Now look at the following chart. You'll see the names of each of the celebrations in the pictures on page 148. Were your guesses correct? Complete the chart with information about the celebrations from "What Is Your Favorite Celebration?" Make a check (✔) in the columns that describe the celebrations.

Celebration	Special Clothing or Costumes	Special Meals or Foods	Presents	Entertainment or Dancing	Decorations
Halloween, United States	✓				
Egyptian Wedding					
Quinceañera, Latin America					
Venice Carnival					
Birthday Party in the United States					

Getting Ready to Read

Before you read, answer this question with a partner:

- What do you already know about Chinese New Year?

As you read, try to answer this question:

- What is the main purpose of Chinese New Year?

Read

Reading 2: Chinese New Year

1 As my non-Chinese husband, Randy, quickly realized, Chinese New Year is a time for big family get-togethers when everyone eats lots of special food. His first taste of Chinese New Year, one February day just after we'd met ten years ago, was a delicious culture shock.[1] At first he was very surprised by the size of my family—30 to 40 aunts and uncles, cousins, nephews, and nieces, plus close family friends—all assembled for an **open house** with a **buffet.** But his shock was softened by all of the brilliant food and fine spirits carefully prepared for all the **banquets,** dinner parties, afternoon teas, and **open houses** that make up the New Year **celebration.** Today, Randy's an expert on Chinese New Year, and he enjoys it more than anyone I know.

2   New Year is based on the Chinese lunar[2] calendar and **marks** the first day of spring. We **celebrate** for two weeks. It's a time of

[1]**culture shock:** the feeling of surprise caused by something from a different culture
[2]**lunar:** having to do with the moon

renewal: We **traditionally** spend the days before the New Year in special activities that will promote a more promising year. It's an exciting time: We thoroughly clean and sweep the house, have our hair cut and washed, pay back debts in full and settle[3] all family quarrels[4]—all to start fresh. It's a time to shop for new clothes, fresh food, fruits and gifts, and to stop at the bank for crisp new bills to stuff into red "lucky money" envelopes that we give to children. These activities cleanse[5] the soul and repel[6] **evil spirits** and misfortune. They **ensure** a year of **prosperity,** success, and good luck.

3   At New Year, we expect friends and relatives to drop in any time for tea and snacks. Randy likes to visit the aunts who make the best **dumplings** and hot appetizers. Auntie Linda is the most **traditional** in my family: She treats us to her crisp spring rolls, sweet pan-fried pudding cakes, sticky sesame balls, and steamed and crisp dumplings.

4   Not all the food set out for New Year is to be eaten—by now, Randy knows not to touch the gorgeous[7] oranges, enormous pomelos,[8] juicy peaches, and fragrant tangerines stacked pyramid-style on flat plates that are displayed throughout the house. We put the fruit plates in special places around the house—on the mantel near an altar,[9] on a shelf in the kitchen, on dressers in the bedroom—for good luck and **longevity.** And we won't eat this fruit until after the **celebrations** are over.

5   At the end of New Year's Day, the New Year **feast** is set out. My mom's New Year dinner is usually an array of **traditional, symbolic** dishes, plus an assortment of family favorites. There is always a **banquet**-style soup—perhaps steamed whole winter melon soup served in its hollowed-out shell, or a lovely bird's nest soup floating in a delicate broth. Out of respect for religion, we also have jai, a Buddhist vegetarian dish. To **emphasize abundance** and wealth, we set out a delicious chicken dish, chopped into bite-sized pieces and served with a green onion-and-ginger dip, and a whole fish in a delicate sauce.

6   It's a dinner not to be missed.

—adapted from "Delicious Symbolism of Chinese New Year," by Joyce Jue

[3]**settle:** solve; end in a positive way
[4]**quarrel:** fight
[5]**cleanse:** make clean
[6]**repel:** push away
[7]**gorgeous:** very beautiful
[8]**pomelos:** large yellow fruits, similar to grapefruit
[9]**altar:** a table on which people offer things to their god(s) or ancestors

◆ **After You Read**

1. What is the main purpose of the Chinese New Year?

2. If you celebrate the Chinese New Year, which of the following do you do? Check (✓) the correct statements.

    _____ Decorate the house with bowls of fruit.

    _____ Have your hair cut.

    _____ Start fights with family members.

    _____ Clean the house.

    _____ Buy new clothes.

    _____ When friends drop in, tell them to go away.

    Now look at the activities you didn't check. Rewrite them to make them correct. Change some of the words in the statements.

    EXAMPLE:

    You *don't* start fights with family members.

3. Match the New Year activities and foods that Jue describes with their meanings. Write the letter of the meaning next to its activity. There may be more than one answer for some activities.

Meanings	Activities
a. Repel evil spirits and misfortune	_____ Eat a special chicken dish
b. Bring prosperity and good luck	_____ Decorate with fruit
c. Ensure longevity	_____ Eat a vegetarian dish
d. Show respect for religion	_____ Clean the house
e. Emphasize abundance	_____ Give money envelopes to children

The Fourth of July (also known as Independence Day) celebrates the birthday of the United States of America. America declared its independence from Britain with the signing of the Declaration of Independence on July 4th 1776. This holiday is usually celebrated with picnics, parades, marching bands, and fireworks.

FROM READING TO WRITING
. . . .

Answer the following questions to prepare for the writing assignment in this chapter. These exercises use the reading selections to teach you about writing.

1. Review Paragraph 4 of "Chinese New Year." Find the descriptive adjectives that the author uses to describe the following:

    _____ oranges   _____ pomelos

    _____ peaches   _____ tangerines

2. Review each of the descriptions in "What Is Your Favorite Celebration?" Find the descriptive adjectives that the speakers use to describe their favorite celebrations.

- This is my favorite celebration because we get to dress up in

  _____ costumes.

- We eat a special food at this time too—a fried pastry

  _____.

- We put _____ lights on the house so everyone would know that a special event was taking place.

- The girl wears a _____ dress.

- People dance all night in the streets in _____ costumes.

3. Find words and expressions in "Chinese New Year" that explain the meaning and purpose of Chinese New Year, New Year food, and activities. List them.

_____

_____

_____

_____

_____

◆ Getting Ready to Write

Describing Celebrations

When you describe and explain a celebration, you need to help your reader understand ideas and activities that may be new to him or her. To do this, organize your ideas in a logical way and use descriptive words and phrases.

Organize Paragraphs Around Main Ideas

Organize the main ideas of your essay into paragraphs. Make sure that each paragraph has only *one* main idea and stays on the topic for the entire paragraph. This helps your reader follow your information.

Here's one way to organize information about a celebration:

1. First Paragraph: Introduction

   Explain the purpose of the celebration and/or its main activities.

2. Next Paragraphs: Body

Give information on the celebration. For example, explain any or all of the following:

- the history of the celebration (why people celebrate it)
- special decorations and their meanings
- special foods and their meanings
- special clothes and their meanings

(You can present these paragraphs in any order, as long as each one has only one main idea.)

3. Last Paragraph: Conclusion

Give your concluding ideas about the celebration. One way to do this is to restate the information in your introduction.

Practice Rewrite your freewrite on page 150. Use the organizational pattern you just learned.

LANGUAGE LEARNING STRATEGY

Apply the Strategy

Study how other writers organize ideas. This will improve your own writing. Look for ways the writer helps you understand the topic. Seeing how someone else's writing is organized will give you ideas about how to organize your own writing assignment.

Make a simple outline of the article about the Chinese New Year. First, list the purpose of each paragraph in the article. Then list the main idea or ideas in each paragraph (except for the conclusion). The outline has been started for you. Fill in the missing information:

I. Purpose: Introduction

Ideas/Examples: _____

_____

_____

(continued on next page)

II. Purpose: Give background

Ideas/Examples: based on lunar calendar

_____

_____

III. Purpose: _____

Ideas/Examples: spring rolls

_____

_____

IV. Purpose: _____

Ideas/Examples: _____

_____

_____

V. Purpose: Explain main activity (banquet) in detail

Ideas/Examples: _____

_____

_____

Use Descriptive Adjectives

As you saw in Chapter 5, using descriptive adjectives and phrases helps give your reader a clear picture of what you are describing. When you use descriptive language in an article about food and decorations, people can really see and almost taste what you're describing.

Practice Review descriptive words and phrases by drawing a line under the descriptive words and phrases in these examples:

1. We put strings of colored lights on the house so everyone would know that a special event was taking place.

2. We eat a special food at this time, too—a fried pastry sprinkled with sugar.

Now rewrite three sentences from your freewrite on page 150. This time, use more (or different) descriptive words and phrases.

Choose a Topic

Choose a celebration you would like to write about. It can be one that you are familiar with or one that is new to you. It can be from your native country or culture, or another country or culture.

Choose a celebration that has at least two of the following:

- Special activities that symbolize or mean something
- A long, traditional history
- Special foods that symbolize or mean something
- Special clothes that symbolize or mean something
- Decorations that symbolize or mean something

Write your idea here:

Name of celebration: _____

Plan Your Writing

Find out more about your celebration. Answer as many of the following questions as you can. If you need help, interview someone at school or go to the library and find books and articles about the celebration you chose.

I. What is the name of the celebration?

What do people usually/traditionally do for this celebration?

What events occur? In what order?

Activities?

Rituals?

Games?

Music? Dances?

Presents?

Meals?

II. What is the celebration's background?

What is its history?

What is it for?

Does it signify a change in anything? (In other words, does it signify a change in someone's life? For example, a marriage ceremony joins two people.)

What does it symbolize? (For example, the Chinese New Year symbolizes renewal and the arrival of spring.)

III. What foods, drinks, or meals are traditionally part of the celebration?

Do they symbolize anything? What?

Do they have a function? (For example, to bring luck?)

IV. What special clothing do people wear for the celebration?

What does the clothing symbolize?

V. What special decorations are used for the celebration?

What do they symbolize? (For example, an evergreen Christmas tree symbolizes life in the dead of winter.)

Now that you have a topic and some ideas, use this outline for organizing the information you just found about your celebration.

Start here:

> I. Introduce your topic

> II. Give background on the celebration

Then choose two or three of the following:

> III. Describe the food prepared for the celebration

> IV. Describe decorations for the celebration

> V. Describe special clothes for the celebration

> VI. Explain the activities involved in the celebration

End with this:

VII. Conclusion

Study an Example

Read this example of a student essay and answer the questions that follow:

My Favorite Celebration

1 I have a lot of favorite celebrations. I think I like all celebrations. For example, I like weddings, New Year's, carnival, and birthdays. But my favorite celebration is New Year's.

2 New Year's for me is special because it's a time to renew my objectives, to rediscover them with high energy. I usually celebrate New Year's with my parents—it's a special time we share together with enthusiasm and joy.

3 In Brazil, we have a lot of New Year's customs. For example, people often dress in white or wear new clothes. Many people celebrate at the beach. We watch fireworks, and people go into the water and jump over twelve waves for good luck in the coming year. An important part of this ritual is to never turn your back to the sea. Another good luck ritual is to take roses to the sea and toss them in.

4 In my family, we don't go to the beach, but we always dress in new clothes. We always eat lentil soup for dinner that night, and always at midnight, we drink champagne. Then we embrace each other, and we always give each other a laurel leaf. It's to bring luck and money in the new year.

5 I like this celebration because people are happy and have high expectations for the new year. I always think that the new year will be better than the last year. So far, this has always happened!

—Ana Paula Issa Kimura

1. What did you like about the student example?

2. Did the writer choose an interesting topic?

3. Did the writer give you a clear picture of the celebration? Did she use descriptive adjectives?

4. Do you have any advice or suggestions for Ana Paula?

ACADEMIC POWER STRATEGY

Apply the Strategy

Study with a partner to help make you a better student and help you enjoy school more. Find another student with whom you can study and discuss ideas. You can also edit each other's writing. This will help you improve your work.

Practice studying with another student. Bring the research notes that you made on your celebration to class. Find a partner and take turns telling each other about the celebration you've chosen. Make sure you give your partner lots of examples of things such as food, activities, and decorations.

Then write a short description of one part of the celebration on your own. You can choose food and its meaning, clothing and its meaning, activities, etc.

When you finish writing, exchange your paper with your partner. Read each other's work and make suggestions. You can use this paragraph and your partner's ideas later, when you write your assignment for this chapter.

 Write

Now you're ready to write. Write about a celebration. Explain the purpose of the celebration. Use the ideas you developed in Choose a Topic and Plan Your Writing on page 163.

After You Write

Revise

Now have someone else read your writing so that you know what to add or take away. Remember that in this stage of the writing process, you are looking at ideas. Exchange your paper with your new study partner to evaluate by answering these questions:

Questions for Revision	Yes	No
1. Did the writer organize each paragraph around one main idea? Notes:		

Questions for Revision	Yes	No
2. In the body paragraphs, does the writer give information on the celebration, for example, the history of the celebration (why people celebrate it)? Special decorations and their meanings? Special foods and their meanings? Special clothes and their meanings? Notes:		
3. Do you have a clear picture of the celebration? Does the writer use descriptive adjectives? Notes:		
4. Would you like to know something else about the celebration? If yes, write down here something the writer should add:		

Plan your revision by reading the checklist. Talk with your teacher or classmates about what you can do to improve this essay. Write some notes in case you choose to rewrite this paper later.

Edit

Now review your writing for correctness. Look at spelling, punctuation, and grammar. Read and respond to this checklist alone; then exchange papers and ask a classmate to answer these questions:

Questions for Editing	Yes	No
1. Does the writer use vocabulary that is specific and correct? Notes:		
2. Has the writer used separable and inseparable phrasal verbs correctly? Notes:		
3. Are there any grammar mistakes you want to point out? If yes, what should the writer check?		

Correct any mistakes your classmate or teacher pointed out in the Editing Checklist. Now you are ready to place your writing in your Writing Portfolio. You may choose to rewrite it or expand it to a longer piece now or later.

PUTTING IT ALL TOGETHER

Use What You Have Learned

Write about another celebration. Use what you learned in this chapter to make your writing interesting and correct. Refer to your teacher's or classmate's comments on your first draft. When you are finished, put your writing in your Writing Portfolio.

Test-Taking Tip

Write an outline before starting to write your answer to an essay test question. Good essay writers spend time coming up with an outline before starting to answer an essay question. Outlining helps you to think the question through, to organize your ideas, to make sure you don't leave out important information, and to check that you have answered the question that was asked.

CHECK YOUR PROGRESS

On a scale of 1 to 5, rate how well you have mastered the goals set at the beginning of the chapter:

1 2 3 4 5   organize paragraphs around main ideas and use descriptive adjectives to write about celebrations.

1 2 3 4 5   review the use of separable and inseparable phrasal verbs.

1 2 3 4 5   look for words and expressions in reading passages that you can use in your own writing.

1 2 3 4 5   study how other writers organize ideas.

1 2 3 4 5   study with a partner.

If you've given yourself a 3 or lower on any of these goals:

- visit the *Tapestry* web site for additional practice.
- ask your instructor for extra help.
- review the sections of the chapter that you found difficult.
- work with a partner or study group to further your progress.

"Good movies make you care, make you believe in possibilities again."

—Pauline Kael

Read the quotation by Pauline Kael. She believes that movies are more than entertainment. Do you agree? Write down a few of your own ideas about what movies can do for people:

_____

_____

_____

_____

GREAT CLASSIC MOVIES

$\mathbf{M}$ovies provide fun and entertainment, and they also say a lot about who we are and how we see ourselves. By thinking about movies and expressing our opinions about them, we can learn a lot about ourselves and our culture. In this chapter, you are going to summarize and give your opinion of a movie.

Setting Goals

In this chapter, you will practice writing an evaluation. Specifically, you will summarize a movie plot, express your opinion, and discuss features such as the acting, the dialogue, and the setting. In order to do this, you will:

- ◈ identify your learning goals before you begin a new lesson.

- ◈ study noun suffixes to expand your writing vocabulary.

- ◈ practice using time clauses with *while* in your writing.

- ◈ read an English-language newspaper or magazine.

- ◈ take notes to prepare for a writing assignment.

LANGUAGE LEARNING STRATEGY

Apply the Strategy

I dentify your learning goals before you begin a new lesson. This helps you focus your learning. Preview the material you are going to study and ask yourself what you hope to learn or what skill you hope to master.

Have you noticed that we ask you to set goals in each chapter? Now preview the readings and exercises in this chapter. What would you like to learn about writing an evaluation of a movie? What would you like to learn about summarizing a movie? What did you learn about writing in previous chapters that you would like to practice or expand on in this chapter? Think of a specific writing goal for you for this chapter and write it here:

_____

_____

◁ Getting Started

In this chapter, you are going to summarize a movie plot and give your opinion of it. You can get started by talking about movies. Answer these questions with a partner:

- What's your favorite movie? What do you like about it?
- Who is your favorite actor? Why?
- What's your favorite kind of movie (for example, drama, comedy, adventure, horror)?
- What movies have you seen recently? What did you think of them?

Now think of your own questions to ask your partner about movies.

MEETING THE TOPIC

Look at the following photos of scenes from classic movies. Classic movies are movies that stay popular for many years. What are the names of these classic movies? Match the titles in the box with the scenes.

A. _____   C. _____   E. _____

B. _____   D. _____

> No form of art goes beyond ordinary consciousness as film does, straight to our emotions, deep into the twilight room of the soul.
>
> —INGRID BERGMAN

Titles		
1. *E.T.*	3. *The Gold Rush*	5. *Lawrence of Arabia*
2. *Casablanca*	4. *Gone with the Wind*	

Give and get information about movies. Write in the following table examples of movie types, titles, actors, and reasons to like movies. For each example that you get from a classmate, give a new one. After you share your information, move on to a new classmate. Try to fill in as much of the following table as you can.

TYPES OF MOVIES	MOVIE TITLES	FAMOUS ACTORS/ACTRESSES	REASONS PEOPLE LIKE MOVIES
comedy	The Gold Rush	Charlie Chaplin	good acting

Freewrite

You've had a chance to look, listen, and talk. Now connect your ideas in writing. Write about your favorite movie. You can write notes or sentences or make a list. Write as quickly as you can. Don't worry about grammar or spelling; just get your ideas on paper.

TUNING IN: "A Scene From a Different Kind of Classic Movie"

A scene from a different kind of classic movie

The CNN video you will watch is about an African American movie producer from the past, Oscar Micheaux. Read the following questions. Then watch the video and answer the questions.

1. What kind of film is *Symbol of the Unconquered*?

   a. A silent film.

   b. A musical.

   c. A science fiction film.

2. When was the film created?

   a. In 1940.

   b. In 1920.

   c. In 1970.

3. What were "race films"?

   a. Movies made by a white or a black producer for all audiences.

   b. Movies made by a white or a black producer for white audiences.

   c. Movies made by a white or a black producer for black audiences.

4. What is the subject of *Symbol of the Unconquered?*

   a. The problems of white people.

   b. The problems of light-skinned blacks

   c. The problems of dark-skinned blacks.

5. How were Micheaux's films different from other "race films" of the time?

   a. He hired white people to play the parts of black characters.

   b. He hired black people to play the parts of black characters.

   c. He hired both white and black people to play the parts of black characters.

EXPANDING YOUR LANGUAGE

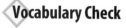

Vocabulary Check

Expand your vocabulary by studying some words and expressions that can be used to talk about movies. Check the words you already know. Work in small groups. Add new words to your Vocabulary Log.

_____ character	_____ director	_____ review
_____ classic movie	_____ hero/heroine	_____ script
_____ costume	_____ location	_____ setting
_____ dialogue	_____ performance	_____ special effects

◆ Vocabulary Tip

Noun Suffixes

In Chapter 4, you saw how knowing stems and affixes can help increase your vocabulary. In this chapter, you'll see some noun suffixes that you can add to verbs. These will expand your writing vocabulary. Look at these examples:

VERB	NOUN: PERSON	NOUN: THING
perform	performer	performance

Some common suffixes that change verbs into nouns are *-or*, *-er*, *-ion*, *-ing*, *-ance*, and *-ence*. Look at some more examples:

VERB	NOUN: PERSON	NOUN: THING
direct	director	direction
act	actor	action, acting
write	writer	writing

◆ Vocabulary Building

1. Practice using word forms. Fill in the blanks in the following paragraph with the correct form of the words in the box. Note: You can use some words more than once.

performer(s)	review	performance(s)	reviewer(s)
direct(ed)	actor(s)	director(s)	

I read a (a) _____ of the new *Alien* movie in the

newspaper. The (b) _____ said that she didn't like

it. She said that the (c) _____ wasn't very good.

She thought this because the (d) _____ was new:

he had never (e) _____ a science fiction movie before,

so he didn't understand how to get the (f) _____ to

give good(g) _____.

2. Rewrite your freewrite. Use five of the words from the Vocabulary Check.

Grammar You Can Use: Time Clauses with *While*

Time clauses let you write about two things that happen at the same time. Time clauses are useful when you write a summary of a movie plot. For example:

- He meets the love of his life *while* crossing the Atlantic on an ocean liner.

This sentence combines two events that happened at the same time:

1. He meets the love of his life.

2. He is crossing the Atlantic on an ocean liner.

You can also put the *while* clause at the beginning of the sentence. When you do this, you separate the two clauses with a comma. Note that sometimes you need to change the order of the clauses to be sure the sentence is logical. For example:

- *While* crossing the Atlantic on an ocean liner, he meets the love of his life.

Note that you don't repeat the subject of the two clauses when you combine them. Here's another example:

Jack is crossing the Atlantic on an ocean liner.

Jack jumps overboard.

- *While* crossing the Atlantic on an ocean liner, Jack jumps overboard.

Combine the following sentences. Use *while*. Write the new sentences using both patterns. Be sure you put the clauses in a logical order.

1. She reads the mysterious letter.

She realizes who the killer is.

_____

_____

_____

2. The dinosaur is chasing the children.

   The dinosaur falls into a deep hole.

   _____

   _____

   _____

3. The detective is interviewing suspects.

   The detective learns that another murder has occurred.

   _____

   _____

   _____

4. She is running across the street.

   She drops the important evidence into the sewer.

   _____

   _____

   _____

5. He is working as a chemist.

   He discovers a new compound.

   _____

   _____

   _____

READING FOR WRITING

One of the best ways to improve your writing is to read other people's work. Read the following selections. In the first selection, people in an interview answer this question: What is your favorite movie? The second selection is a movie review of *The Wizard of Oz* from a web site.

Getting Ready to Read

As you read, answer these questions:

- What movies do these people like? Why do they like them?

Read

Reading 1: What Is Your Favorite Movie?

1. *Judy, English teacher, 42 years old:*

   Laurie: What's your favorite movie?

   Judy: My favorite movie? It's got to be *The Wizard of Oz.*

   Laurie: Why?

   Judy: What I like best about *The Wizard of Oz* is the **characters**—the Scarecrow, the Cowardly Lion, and the Tin Woodsman. I also like the story. It has a nice message: "There's no place like home."

2. *Sam, student, 7 years old:*

   Laurie: Sam, what's your favorite movie?

   Sam: My favorite movie is *E.T.*

   Laurie: What do you like about *E.T.*, Sam?

   Sam: It's got great **special effects**! I like the part where the boy's bicycle flies in the air! I wish my bike would fly in the air like that!

3. *Joy, clothing designer, 24 years old:*

   Laurie: Joy, would you mind telling me what your favorite movie is?

   Joy: Sure. It's *Gone with the Wind.*

   Laurie: What do you like about it?

   Joy: It shows the way life in the southern United States used to be. That's interesting to me. I also love the **costumes.**

4. *Mike, chef, 30 years old:*

   Laurie: What's your favorite movie?

   Mike: I guess it's *Lawrence of Arabia.*

   Laurie: What do you like about it?

   Mike: Well, I like the story and the desert scenes. I also think the acting is great. Peter O'Toole is great in that movie.

After You Read

1. What two things does Judy like about *The Wizard of Oz*?

2. What does Sam like about *E.T.*?

3. What does Joy love about *Gone with the Wind*?

4. What two things does Mike like about *Lawrence of Arabia*?

◇Getting Ready to Read

Before you read the movie review, discuss the movie with a partner. Discuss your answers to these questions:

- Have you seen *The Wizard of Oz*?
- What is the plot?
- Who are the characters?
- Where does the movie take place?
- Who are the actors?
- Do you like it? Why or why not?

◇Read

Reading 2: The Wizard of Oz Returns

1　Join Dorothy once again on her magical journey in the land of Oz! The new version of *The Wizard of Oz* is better than ever, this time with improved color and sound. In this wonderful American fairy tale, a young girl named Dorothy (Judy Garland) learns an important lesson: As she says, "There's no place like home." Dorothy lives on a farm in Kansas. One day, a large tornado picks up Dorothy, her house, and her dog, and drops them in the land of Oz. Things in Oz are strange and beautiful, but Dorothy just wants to get back home. The Good Fairy of the North helps her, but the Wicked Witch of the West is trying to capture her because she blames Dorothy for the death of her sister, the Wicked Witch of the East. While trying to find her way home, Dorothy meets the Scarecrow, who needs a brain, the Tin Man, who needs a heart, and the Cowardly Lion, who needs courage.

2　　I like *The Wizard of Oz*. It has everything that makes a movie a **classic**: a wonderful story, good **special effects,** and memorable music. Based on the American fairy tale by Frank Baum, *The Wizard of Oz* contains all the elements of a great story: good and bad witches, magic, a **heroine** with many obstacles, and lovable **characters** who help her achieve her goal. The special effects remain impressive, even after all these years: the scene with the army of flying monkeys still makes my hair stand on end.[1] The highlight,[2] though, is the unforgettable music, including such songs as "Somewhere Over the Rainbow" and "Follow the Yellow Brick Road." Don't miss this opportunity to see *The Wizard of Oz* the way it was meant to be seen: on the big screen.

[1]**makes my hair stand on end:** scares me
[2]**highlight:** best part

◆**After You Read**

1. What is the plot of *The Wizard of Oz*? Describe it in your own words.

2. Who are some of the characters?

3. Where does the story take place? What is this place like?

4. What is the name of one actor?

5. Does the reviewer like the movie? Give three reasons that support your answer.

FROM READING TO WRITING

Answer the following questions about the review of *The Wizard of Oz* to prepare for the writing assignment in this chapter. These exercises use the reading selection to teach you about writing.

1. Where does the reviewer tell you what the movie is about, in the first paragraph or in the second?

2. Where does the reviewer give her opinion of the movie, in the first paragraph or in the second?

3. What does the movie title look like in the article? What kind of punctuation did she use?

4. Does the reviewer quote any dialogue from the movie? What kind of punctuation did she use?

◆**Getting Ready to Write**   **Evaluating a Movie**

A good movie review has two main parts: a summary of the movie and the writer's opinion of the movie. When the movie title is mentioned, it's underlined or italicized. The review can also refer to the actors and include quotations of interesting dialogue from the movie.

LANGUAGE LEARNING STRATEGY

Read an English-language newspaper or magazine at least once a week to make your writing more fluent. It will help you learn vocabulary and sentence structures to use in your writing. It will also give you ideas for writing assignments.

Apply the Strategy

Find a movie review in a newspaper or a magazine. Try *USA Today* (newspaper) or *U.S. News & World Report* (magazine). Read the review. As you read, look for ideas and vocabulary that you can use in the writing assignment for this chapter. Take notes on your reading—you may want to use them later.

The five greatest American films of all time, according to the American Film Institute:
1. **Citizen Kane (1941)**
2. **Casablanca (1942)**
3. **The Godfather (1972)**
4. **Gone with the Wind (1939)**
5. **Lawrence of Arabia (1962)**

Summarizing a Movie Plot

To summarize a movie plot, you discuss only the main points or events of the story. You present these events in the order that they happened. You write in the present tense. You describe the main characters and the actors who play them. You can also talk about the main location(s) where the story takes place, but you omit most of the other details. Don't write too much: A paragraph (six to ten sentences) is usually enough to give the summary of a movie plot.

Practice Practice writing a movie summary. Work with a partner. Pick a movie. Pick one that you discussed at the beginning of this chapter, or another one that you both know. Follow these steps:

1. List the main events of the movie in order. What happens first? What happens next? And so on.

2. List the main characters and the actors who play them.

Talking About Characters and the Actors Who Play Them

When you talk about the characters in a movie, it's a good idea to name the actors who play them. Here are some ways you can do this:

- Put the actor's name in parentheses after the character's name: "While trying to find her way home, she meets the Cowardly Lion (Burt Lahr)."
- Use "played by" after the character's name: "While trying to find her way home, she meets the Cowardly Lion, played by Burt Lahr."

---

3. Describe the main location(s).

Now combine the sentences into a paragraph. When you finish, answer these questions about your paragraph:

- How long is your paragraph?
- Did you mention only the main characters and locations?
- Did you describe the events in order?

Expressing Your Opinion

When you express your opinion about a movie, you say whether or not you liked it, and why. Here are two examples:

- I liked   *Gone with the Wind*   because the acting is great.
- I didn't like *Gone with the Wind*   because the story is unrealistic.

Notice the reasons for liking or disliking a movie:

the *acting* is *great*

the *story* is *unrealistic*

When you give your opinion, you can talk about the actors (or the acting), the director, the music, the special effects, and so on. It's a good idea to use descriptive adjectives when you discuss what you like and dislike about movies.

Practice

1. Work in small groups. Take turns. Fill in as many blanks as you can; then pass the chart to your neighbor. Continue until you have filled in the chart.

LIST A: NAMES OF MOVIES YOU'VE SEEN	LIST B: THING TO HAVE AN OPINION ABOUT	LIST C: ADJECTIVES
Gone with the Wind	the acting	_____
The Wizard of Oz	the setting	magical
E.T.	the story	uninteresting
_____	the theme music	_____
_____	the dialogue	_____
_____	the amount of violence	_____
_____	_____	_____
_____	_____	_____

2. Now take turns expressing your opinion. Use ideas from the lists in Item 1.

EXAMPLE:

I didn't like/I liked _____ (*Batman*) _____ (List A) because the _____ (*costumes*) _____ (List B) is/are
_____ (*great/ugly*) _____ (List C).

Punctuate the Title Correctly

Always include the title of the movie in your review. You must itali-
cize or underline it.

EXAMPLES:

Lawrence of Arabia	or	Lawrence of Arabia
The Seven Samurai	or	The Seven Samurai
Gone with the Wind	or	Gone with the Wind
Casablanca	or	Casablanca

Notice also that you must capitalize all the "important" words in a
movie title. You don't capitalize words such as *the* or *with* (for example, in *Gone with the Wind*) unless they are at the beginning of
the title.

Practice Correct the titles in the following sentences:

1. I like Gone with the wind because it shows the way life in the
   southern United States used to be.

2. My favorite movie is Lawrence Of Arabia because Peter O'Toole
   is great in that movie.

3. Have you ever seen the movie of mice and men? It's based on a
   John Steinbeck novel.

4. Sam Shepard is great in The Right Stuff.

5. The special effects in godzilla weren't very exciting.

Quoting Dialogue from the Movie

If you quote lines from a movie, use a comma or a colon to separate
the quotation from the person who said it. You must use quotation
marks around the quotation.

> The screen is a magic medium. It has such power that it can retain interest as it conveys emotions and moods that no other art form can hope to tackle.
>
> —STANLEY KUBRICK

EXAMPLE:

As Dorothy says at the end of the movie, "There's no place like home."

Practice Correct the quotations in these sentences:

1. I like the part where Clint Eastwood says go ahead, make my day in *Dirty Harry*.

2. Everyone loves Arnold Schwartzenegger's line I'll be back in *The Terminator*.

Choose a Topic

Make a list of movies to see and review. Look at current newspapers and magazines for ideas. Choose one to watch. (You can either go to a movie theater or rent a video.)

ACADEMIC POWER STRATEGY

Apply the Strategy

Take good notes on information that you watch or read in preparation for writing. Taking notes helps you focus on the material. It also gives you vocabulary and ideas that you can use later in your writing.

With a partner, see the movie you chose in Choose a Topic. Take notes or be prepared to take notes immediately afterward. (Hint: If you rent a movie, you can stop and rewind it to see important or difficult parts over again. You also have more light to take notes, and can talk to your partner without bothering anybody.)

Plan Your Writing

Back in class, work in small groups. Discuss the film you saw with your group. As you discuss your film, summarize it and express your opinion about it. Now find someone who saw the same movie as you. It can be your partner, or someone new. Fill in Part A of the following chart together. Then fill in Part B by yourself.

Part A: Summary
Title of Movie:
Plot (List of Main Points):

Part B: Review
Opinion:
Reason 1 (the acting, the dialogue, etc.)
Reason 2
Reason 3
Restatement of Opinion: (Note: Paraphrase it. [Say it in different words.])

After you fill in the chart, write a one-paragraph summary of the plot of the movie. Do this alone. Then compare your summary with your partner's. Did you leave anything out? Rewrite it if you think you can make it better.

Study an Example

Read the following excerpt from a student's movie review. It's the opinion part of the review. Then answer the questions that follow.

I didn't like *Terminator II*. The main reason is that it is simply too violent. The characters are constantly shooting people and blowing up buildings. They're supposed to be angry about something, but you never know exactly what they're angry about. The reason for the violence is not clear, so it seems excessively cruel. Violence that has no motivation is also extremely uninteresting. So I would say that *Terminator II* is a bad movie because it is boring.

—Kelvin Yee

1. Is the writer's opinion clearly stated? What is his conclusion about the violence in *Terminator II*?

2. What did you like about the student example?

3. Do you have any advice or suggestions for Kelvin?

 Write

Write a movie review. Summarize the movie you saw and express your opinion about it. Use the organization chart you made on page 185. Remember to use quotations correctly and to use the present tense.

After You Write

Revise

Now have someone else read your writing so that you know what to add or take away. Remember that in this stage of the writing process, you are looking at ideas. Exchange your paper with a classmate or give your paper to your teacher, your mentor, or a friend to evaluate by answering these questions:

Questions for Revision	Yes	No
1. Is the plot summary clear? Notes:		
2. Does the writer clearly state his or her opinion of the movie? Notes:		
3. Does the writer give reasons or examples to support his or her opinion? Notes:		

Plan your revision by reading the evaluation. Talk with your teacher or classmates about what you can do to improve this essay. Write some notes in case you choose to rewrite this paper later.

Edit

Now review your writing for correctness. Look at spelling, punctuation, and grammar. Read and respond to this checklist alone; then exchange papers and ask a classmate to answer these questions:

Questions for Editing	Yes	No
1. Does the writer use vocabulary that is specific and correct? Notes:		
2. Does the writer use correct punctuation for the title and any quoted dialogue? Notes:		
3. Does the writer use any time clauses with *while*? Are they correct? Notes:		
4. Are there any grammar mistakes you want to point out? If yes, what should the writer check?		

Correct any mistakes your classmate or teacher pointed out in the Editing Checklist. Now you are ready to place your writing in your Writing Portfolio. You may want to rewrite it or expand it to a longer piece later.

PUTTING IT ALL TOGETHER

Use What You Have Learned

Write a review about another movie. Or write about a play or a musical event. Use what you have learned in this chapter to make your writing interesting and correct. Refer to your teacher's or classmate's comments on your first draft. When you are finished, put your writing in your Writing Portfolio.

Test-Taking Tip

Use the right level of language when writing essay exam answers. While you may be concerned about using language that is too simple, it is important not to use language that is overly complicated. Using overly complicated language will rarely impress your instructor as it often leads to the misuse of words and, ultimately, a confusing essay. It is better to use language that you feel comfortable with, as you will be more likely to express yourself more clearly.

CHECK YOUR PROGRESS

On a scale of 1 to 5, rate how well you have mastered the goals set at the beginning of the chapter:

1 2 3 4 5   summarize a movie plot, express your opinion, and discuss features such as the acting, the dialogue, and the setting.

1 2 3 4 5   identify your learning goals before you begin a new lesson.

1 2 3 4 5   study noun suffixes to expand your writing vocabulary.

1 2 3 4 5   practice using time clauses with *while* in your writing.

1 2 3 4 5   read an English-language newspaper or magazine.

1 2 3 4 5   take notes to prepare for a writing assignment.

If you've given yourself a 3 or lower on any of these goals:

- visit the *Tapestry* web site for additional practice.

- ask your instructor for extra help.

- review the sections of the chapter that you found difficult.

- work with a partner or study group to further your progress.

"The only thing that makes civilization go forward is the responsibility of individuals . . . for the species, for the culture, for the larger thing outside ourselves."

—Wallace Stegner

Read the quotation by Wallace Stegner. What do you think he means? Do you agree? Write down the names of a few individuals who have made "civilization go forward":

_____

_____

_____

_____

HIGHLIGHTS OF THE TWENTIETH CENTURY

9

Who were the important people of the twentieth century? What were the important events of the twentieth century? How did these people and events contribute to the world we know today? Reflecting on the past helps us plan for the future. In this chapter, you are going to describe an important person or event from the past.

Setting Goals

In this chapter, you will describe a person or event. Specifically, you will describe an important event or person from the twentieth century. You will state the main idea (the reason the person or event was important), give background on the person or event, and support your main idea with examples, facts, or statistics. In order to do this, you will:

◈ review various past forms, including irregular verbs.

◈ practice using cause and result expressions in your writing.

◈ use a variety of sources for supporting information.

What additional goals do you have for this chapter? Write them here:

_____

_____

◆**Getting Started**

In this chapter, you are going to describe a past event and evaluate it. To get started, discuss these questions with a partner:

- What were some of the most important events of the twentieth century?

- Who were some of the most important people of the twentieth century?

MEETING THE TOPIC

Look at the photos of events and people from the twentieth century. Who or what does each photo show? Take notes on the lines following the photos.

A.

B.

C.

D.

E.

F.

G.

H.

A. _____

_____

B. _____

_____

C. _____

_____

D. _____

_____

E. _____

_____

F. _____

_____

G. _____

_____

H. _____

_____

Give and get information about important people and events of the twentieth century. Use the following chart. Write examples of events and people in different categories. For each example that you get from a classmate, give a new one. After you share your information, move on to a new classmate. Try to fill in as much of the chart as you can.

People	Events
Arts: Picasso	Political Change: World War I
Science: Albert Einstein	Social Change: equal rights for women
Politics: Indira Gandhi	Discoveries: DNA
Religion/Philosophy: Dalai Lama	Natural Disasters: eruption of Mt. Pinatubo
Other:	Other:

Freewrite

You've had a chance to look, listen, and talk. Now connect your ideas in writing. Write about the most important person or event of the twentieth century, in your opinion. Write about more than one, if you wish. You can write notes or sentences or make a list. Write as quickly as you can. Don't worry about grammar or spelling; just get your ideas on paper.

TUNING IN: "Stamps of the Century"

© CNN

Stamps of the Century

The CNN video you will watch is about United States Postal Service stamps that reflect the twentieth century. First, read the questions. Then watch the video and answer the questions.

1. Which stamps were some of the biggest sellers for the U.S. Postal Service, according to the announcer?

   _____

2. Who chose the designs for the Stamps of the Century?

   a. The U.S. Postal Service.

   b. The U.S. government.

   c. The public.

3. Which of the following do Americans *want* to remember, according to the postal survey?

   a. The Brooklyn Dodgers.

   b. The assassination of John F. Kennedy.

   c. The Cold War.

4. Which of the following *don't* Americans want to commemorate, according to the survey?

   a. The Cold War.

   b. Elvis Presley.

   c. The Brooklyn Dodgers.

5. Which of the following describes the 1970s, according to the video?

   a. Bad music.

   b. Band music.

   c. Great fashions.

6. Which statement reflects the announcer's thoughts on the difference between history and memory?

    a. History is what we remember; memories are the truth.

    b. History is what we've lived through; memories are the history we choose to remember.

    c. History is what we choose to remember.

EXPANDING YOUR LANGUAGE

◇ Vocabulary Check

Expand your vocabulary by studying some words and expressions that are used to talk about important people or events of the past. Check the words you already know. Work in small groups. Add new words to your Vocabulary Log.

> **We live in the present, we dream of the future, but we learn eternal truths from the past.**
>
> **—MADAME CHIANG**

_____ ability	_____ potential
_____ contribution	_____ significant
_____ courage	_____ social change
_____ development	_____ to accomplish
_____ discovery	_____ to contribute
_____ dramatically	_____ to owe something to somebody
_____ environment	_____ to shape
_____ political change	_____ to stand out

◇ Vocabulary Tip

Adjective and Adverb Suffixes

In Chapter 8, you saw some noun suffixes that you can add to verbs. In this chapter, you'll see some adjective and adverb suffixes. These will expand your writing vocabulary. Look at the following examples.

environment (noun) → environment**al** (adjective) → environment**ally** (adverb)

Some twentieth century inventions have caused new *environmental* problems.

Many people became more *environmentally* aware in the twentieth century.

Following are some common adjective and adverb suffixes and their usual meanings.

Suffix	Example	Usual Meaning	Part of Speech
-ment	environment	cause, means, result	noun
-al	environmental	having the qualities of	adjective
-ly	environmentally	in this manner	adverb
-ist	scientist	one who is employed in (usually, a particular field)	noun
-ism	communism	action, state, condition	noun
-tion	contribution	condition	noun
-able	profitable	capable of being	adjective
-ity	ability	the quality of or being an example of	noun
-ic	scientific	the quality or condition of	adjective
-ology	biology	science, the study of	noun

Here are some more examples:

NOUN	ADJECTIVE	ADVERB
drama	dramatic	dramatically
profit	profitable	profitably
science	scientific	scientifically
politics	political	politically

Vocabulary Building

1. Complete the blanks in the following sentences with the correct form of the word in parentheses.

   a. (science) One of the greatest _____ discoveries of the twentieth century was DNA.

   b. (politics) Many young Americans became interested in _____ during the Vietnam war.

   c. (drama) The invention of the birth control pill in the 1960s had a _____ effect on American society.

> d. (profit) Collecting baseball cards was a _____ hobby during the 1990s.
>
> e. (drama) Immigration to the United States increased _____ during the early part of the twentieth century.

2. Rewrite your freewrite using at least five words from the Vocabulary Check.

Grammar You Can Use: Review of Past Forms

You will use a variety of past forms when you describe the background or history of important people or events of the twentieth century. To do this, review the simple past, the present perfect, the past continuous, and irregular verbs in these forms. Review past forms by correcting the underlined mistakes in the following paragraph. Write the correct forms on the lines on the next page.

In 1955, Rosa Parks was arrested in Montgomery, Alabama for refusing to give up her seat on a bus to a white man. This event sparked the civil rights movement, which was led by Martin Luther King, Jr.

Hillary Rodham Clinton

Hillary Diane Rodham (1) <u>has been born</u> in Chicago, Illinois, on October 26, 1947. The daughter of Dorothy Rodham and the late Hugh Rodham, she and her two younger brothers, Hugh and Tony, (2) <u>growed up</u> in Park Ridge, Illinois, as part of a close-knit family. Early in life, she (3) <u>learn</u> the importance of commitment to family, work, and service. It is this commitment and the belief that we "all have an obligation to give something of ourselves to our community" that (4) <u>had helped</u> to shape her role and actions as our nation's First Lady. As a young student, Hillary (5) <u>organizes</u> food drives, (6) <u>serves</u> in student government, and (7) <u>was being</u> a member of the National Honor Society. She was a member of the local Methodist youth group, and was also a Girl Scout. After graduating from Wellesley College in 1969, Hillary enrolled in Yale Law School, where she developed her strong concern for protecting the interests of children and families, and (8) <u>meeted</u> Bill Clinton, a fellow law student. Hillary (9) <u>was marrying</u> Bill Clinton in 1975.

—adapted from web site "The First Lady's Biography":
http://www.whitehouse.gov/WH/EOP/
First_Lady/html/HILLARY_Bio.html

1. _____
2. _____
3. _____
4. _____
5. _____
6. _____
7. _____
8. _____
9. _____

◆ Grammar You Can Use: Cause and Result Expressions

In this chapter, you are going to explain the reason a person or event from the twentieth century was important. To do this, you may have to discuss the results of actions, developments, discoveries, or policies. In your writing, it's important to show the difference between the cause of something and its result. Here are expressions that introduce causes:

• because of Many teenagers felt freer to express themselves *because of* Elvis Presley's music.   Result   Cause
• due to Many teenagers felt freer to express themselves *due to* Elvis Presley's music.   Result   Cause

Here are some expressions that introduce results:

• as a result Tim Berners-Lee invented the Internet in 1989. *As a result,* the average person can access information on any subject from around the world in a matter of minutes.	Cause Result
• resulted in The discovery of DNA in the 1950s *resulted in* the development of genetic engineering. Cause Result	
• the result is/was (that) Tim Berners-Lee created the Internet. *The result is that* the average person can access information on any subject from around the world in a matter of minutes.	Cause Result

Practice writing cause and result statements by rewriting your freewrite, page 194. Use at least two of these cause/result expressions.

READING FOR WRITING

One of the best ways to improve your writing is to read other people's work. Through reading models, you can get ideas about the topic and learn how other writers describe the past. The first selection is a short article about a famous person of the twentieth century: Elvis Presley. The second is about a famous event of the twentieth century: the discovery of DNA.

Getting Ready to Read

Before you read, answer these questions:

- When was Elvis Presley particularly popular? Why was he popular?

As you read, answer this question:

- Why was Elvis Presley an important person, in the writer's opinion?

Read

Reading 1: Elvis Presley

1   I was about 10 the first time I heard Elvis. I was walking past this little soda shop, and I saw all of these teenagers inside having fun. All the kids were talking and laughing and having a good time, when all of a sudden this music came on the jukebox.[1] Well, everybody immediately stopped what they were doing and started dancing and jumping around. I'll never forget the energy in that place. It was fantastic. After the song ended, I turned to the girl next to me and asked, "Who was that?" She looked at me as if I was from another planet and said just one word: "Elvis."

2   When I saw that Elvis had the kind of **courage** to dance and love his music and shake his hips, it helped me because if he could feel free inside and dance and shake around, so could I.

[1]**jukebox:** a machine that plays records, usually found in a public place such as a restaurant

In the 50s, we were supposed to do what we were told, which didn't really allow for much freedom. But, like me, a lot of teenagers wanted to be able to find things out for ourselves: who we were inside, what we liked, what we wanted to do. Rock 'n roll music was music from the heart and the soul that gave us a feeling of freedom.

—Bunny Gibson

After You Read

1. What age group liked Elvis Presley?

2. What did Bunny see people doing when they heard Elvis Presley's music?

3. Describe how American teenagers in the 1950s were supposed to behave, according to Bunny.

4. How did Elvis Presley's music (rock 'n roll) make teenagers feel?

5. What music did you like as a teenager? How did it make you feel?

Getting Ready to Read

Before you read, answer these questions:

- What is DNA?

- What is genetic engineering?

As you read, answer this question:

- Why does the writer think that the discovery of DNA and the development of genetic engineering are the most important events of the twentieth century?

Read

Reading 2: Genetic Engineering

1 One of the most important events of the twentieth century was the **discovery** of DNA, which led to the **development** of genetic engineering. Genetic engineering stands out as a **significant** twentieth-century event because it may allow us to end disease, hunger, and pollution.

2   Although genetic engineering, as we know it today, is a relatively new science, for thousands of years, breeders of plants and animals have used breeding methods to produce better combinations of genes. We **owe** the success of modern technologies to the **discovery** of the structure of DNA (deoxyribonucleic acid) by biologists James D. Watson and Francis H. C. Crick in 1953. Because of their **discovery,** scientists developed techniques for altering genes (the hereditary material that determines the characteristics of all living things) or combinations of genes in

an organism.[1] By changing an organism's genes, scientists were able to give organisms and their descendants[2] different traits.[3]

3   In the 1970s and 1980s, scientists developed ways to isolate individual genes and reintroduce them into cells or into plants, animals, or other organisms. In 1982, insulin became the first genetically engineered drug approved by the U.S. Food and Drug Administration for use on people with diabetes. Also in the 1980s, geneticists injected a human-growth hormone gene into mice, and the mice grew to twice their normal size. In 1987, scientists introduced a gene from a bacterial cell into tomato plants, making the plants resistant to caterpillars.

4   It is clear that the discovery of DNA and the subsequent development of genetic engineering techniques have **dramatically** changed our view of life and our **ability** to influence human health and the **environment.** For example, many people suffer from diseases caused by genetic defects. Genetic engineering techniques allow doctors to insert normal genes into the cells of a patient with a hereditary disease to treat the disorder.[4] Disorders that people have suffered and died from for centuries, such as cancer and cystic fibrosis, may now be eliminated.

5   In addition, scientists have engineered special genes into corn, tomato, and soybean plants to make them resistant to disease. Improving the quality of food plants may lead to an end in world hunger. Genetic engineering also has **potential** in controlling pollution. Researchers are developing genetically engineered microorganisms that break down garbage, toxic substances, and other wastes.

◈ **After You Read**

1. What is DNA?

2. What is genetic engineering?

3. Briefly describe the history of genetic engineering.

4. Why does the writer think that the discovery of DNA and the development of genetic engineering are the most important events of the twentieth century?

5. Do you agree that the development of genetic engineering was one of the most important events of the twentieth century? Why or why not?

---

[1]**organism:** a living thing, e.g., a plant or an animal
[2]**descendants:** children or offspring
[3]**traits:** characteristics
[4]**disorder:** disease, illness

6. What other scientific discoveries or developments on the twentieth century were important? Why were they important?

7. Use your knowledge of suffixes to complete the following chart for words related to *gene*:

Word	Meaning	Part of Speech
gene	hereditary material that determines the characteristics of all living things	noun
geneticist		
genetic		
genetically		

8. Most of the early work in the development of genetic engineering happened near the end of the twentieth century. Scan the reading passage. Look for the dates that match the events in the following list:

YEAR	EVENT
_____	Insulin became the first genetically engineered drug approved by the Federal Drug Administration.
_____	Geneticists injected a human-growth hormone gene into mice.
_____	Watson and Crick discovered the structure of DNA.

FROM READING TO WRITING

In 1957, the Soviet Union launched the first man-made satellite, Sputnik, into orbit around Earth.

Answer the following questions to prepare for the writing assignment for this chapter. These exercises use the reading selections to teach you about writing.

1. In which paragraph does Bunny Gibson explain why Elvis Presley was an important person? State in your own words the importance of Elvis Presley and rock music to teenagers like Bunny:

_____

_____

2. Find the descriptive words and phrases in "Elvis Presley" that Bunny Gibson uses to describe the following:

the kids in the soda shop: _____

_____

the energy in the soda shop: _____

_____

Elvis's behavior: _____

_____

3. In which paragraph of "Genetic Engineering" does the author state the importance of genetic engineering?

_____

4. Does the author of "Genetic Engineering" give the history of genetic engineering? If so, in which paragraph(s)?

_____

5. What is the topic of the fourth paragraph of "Genetic Engineering"? Write it here:

_____

6. What is the topic of the fifth paragraph of "Genetic Engineering"? Write it here:

_____

7. Find facts, statistics, and examples in "Genetic Engineering" that answer the following:

Who discovered DNA? _____

_____

When was DNA discovered? _____

_____

What kind of diseases might genetic engineering techniques eliminate?

_____

_____

How can genetic engineering help control pollution?

_____

_____

◆ **Getting Ready to Write**

Writing About an Important Person or Event from the Past

You are going to write about a person or event from the past. You are going to state your main idea: why this person or event was important or how this person or event affected or contributed to the world we live in today. You will include background on your subject, and you will include specific examples of how or why the person or event was important.

State Your Main Idea

State your main idea clearly and state it early in your essay. This helps your reader know what to expect. One way to state a main idea for this kind of essay is with *because*. In other words, say *why* the person or event is or was important in your statement. For example:

- Genetic engineering stands out as a significant twentieth-century event *because* it may allow us to end disease, hunger, and pollution.

When you write this kind of main idea statement, make sure that you can ask yourself a question like this one:

- Question: Why is genetic engineering important?
- Answer: Because it may allow us to end disease, hunger, and pollution.

Practice Think about the people and events you discussed in Getting Started. Choose two people and two events, and write main idea statements for each. Make sure you write a "because" statement. Then exchange your statements with a partner. Ask "why" questions about each other's statements. If you can't give a good answer, rewrite your statement.

Give the Background or History of the Person or Event

Organize your writing for this kind of assignment so that you give background information on your subject. One or two paragraphs are enough, and they should come at the beginning of your essay.

Practice Take one of the people you discussed in Meeting the Topic and write a paragraph about his or her background.

LANGUAGE LEARNING STRATEGY

Use a variety of sources when you need facts, examples, details, or statistics to support your ideas in writing. Your writing will be more accurate and interesting to readers if you use a variety of sources. Possible sources include

- library books on your subject
- newspaper and magazine articles on your subject*
- reference books (some of these include encyclopedias and biographical references such as *Who's Who*)
- web sites

Apply the Strategy

Use at least two of the sources listed above to find facts about one of the people you discussed in Meeting the Topic.

Support Your Main Idea with Examples, Details, Facts, or Statistics

Support your main idea in your body paragraphs with specific examples, details, facts, or statistics. Here are some ways to do this.

To describe a person, you can give examples of his or her behavior, character, interests, activities, or accomplishments.

EXAMPLE: Hillary Clinton was an important person in American history because she had a strong concern for protecting the interests of children and families.

To describe an event, you can give facts and statistics by answering *wh-* questions such as *who, what, when, where, why, how*.

EXAMPLE: We owe the success of modern technologies (what) to the discovery of the structure of DNA (what) by biologists James D. Watson and Francis H. C. Crick (who) in 1953 (when).

Practice Rewrite your freewrite to include examples, facts, details, or statistics about your subject.

In 1961, under the direction of the Soviet Union, East Berlin was separated from West Berlin by a concrete wall, imprisoning its citizens and dividing Germany into two separate and very unequal countries.

*Note: You can find these by using the *Reader's Guide to Periodical Literature* at the library. You can also sometimes find these on the Web.

Choose a Topic

To choose a topic, go back to the chart you filled in for Meeting the Topic, page 192. Work with a partner. Choose the three people or events from the chart that interest you the most and discuss with your partner why these events or people were so important.

LANGUAGE LEARNING STRATEGY

Apply the Strategy

Fill in a chart as you brainstorm for ideas for your writing. This will help you see what you know and don't know about a topic. It will also help you organize ideas for writing.

Take notes in the following chart as you brainstorm with your partner for information on important people and events of the twentieth century.

Person/Event	Why Important?	Examples

ACADEMIC POWER STRATEGY

Choose what interests you the most whenever you have a choice of assignments. Many people do their best work when they are truly interested in the topic. You can't always choose your own topic in school, but whenever you can, choose something that you are interested in, have experience with, or are simply fascinated by.

Apply the Strategy

When you are finished talking about the three people or events, look at your chart. Choose the person or event that you enjoyed discussing the most. This will be the topic of your essay. Write your choice on the following line:

Essay Topic: _____

Plan Your Writing

Now you are ready to plan your writing assignment. Complete the following outline to help you plan:

I. Introduction

State your main idea: _____

_____

(person or event) was the most important person/event of the twentieth century because

_____

_____

II. Describe the history of or background on the person or event:

Person: Who was the person, and what did he or she do?

_____

_____

_____

_____

_____

Event: Answer *wh-* questions: *who, what, when, where, why, how*

_____

_____

_____

_____

_____

III. Give examples of how or why the person or event was so important. (Causes/Results):

Person: What were his or her influences? What changed because of his or her actions?

_____

_____

_____

_____

_____

Event: What were the effects of the event? What happened as a result of this event?

_____

_____

_____

_____

_____

Study an Example

Read this example of a student's essay. Then answer the questions that follow.

Virginia Woolf
. . . .

1 To me, Virginia Woolf is the most important person of the twentieth century. I have chosen her because, even though she was born in the nineteenth century, her writings inspired several generations of twentieth-century feminists.

2 Virginia Woolf was born in London, England, on January 25, 1882. She was born into a family of readers. Her father had a large library, which Virginia had free run of. Since Virginia didn't attend school, this library became a more-than-adequate substitute for a public school and university education. In fact, reading her father's books gave Virginia a different perspective on the world than her more formally educated peers received.

3 Virginia had long considered herself a writer. In 1905 she began to write for publication for the *Times Literary Supplement*. She wrote fiction from 1912 to 1941. Her thirty-year career was often interrupted by serious illness, and by the demands of

family and friends. During this time, she also wrote works of literary criticism and social comment. This work gave her the opportunity to express her feminist ideas. Her thesis was that women should seek what they really want from life and not conform to what society expected of them. Over the years, her ideas have inspired many women to fulfill their desires.

4   I will always remember something that I learned about Virginia Woolf when I studied her in school in Taiwan. She said that if Shakespeare had had a sister, his sister would never have had the same chance to be a writer because she had no right to read or go to school. All she could do was stay at home, care for the household, and marry a wealthy person when she reached a certain age. She couldn't choose what she wanted to do. This was not only true for Shakespeare's sister; it was true for lots of women everywhere.

5   Virginia Woolf wasn't angry; she didn't blame men directly. Rather, she used subtle irony in her work to make her points. In this way, she influenced women of the twentieth century all over the world and helped change the way they think. That is why she is an important person from the twentieth century.

—Prior Huang

In 1997, Scottish scientists announced the successful cloning of a sheep named "Dolly."

1. What did you like about the student example?

2. Has the writer given the background on the person? Has the writer given examples of how or why the person was so important?

3. Do you have any advice or suggestions for Prior?

Write

Now you're ready to write. Write about the most important person or event of the twentieth century. Give the history or the background of the person or the event. Use descriptive adjectives or answers to *wh-* questions. Give examples that show the results of the event or of the person's actions.

After You Write

Revise

Now have someone else read your writing so that you know what to add or take away. Remember that in this stage of the writing process, you are looking at ideas. Exchange your paper with a classmate or give your paper to your teacher, your mentor, or a friend to evaluate by answering the questions on the next page.

Questions for Revision	Yes	No
1. Has the writer stated clearly why the person or event is the most important of the twentieth century? Notes:		
2. Has the writer given the history of or the background on the event or person? Notes:		
3. Has the writer given specific examples of how or why the person or event was so important? Notes:		

Plan your revision by reading the checklist. Talk with your teacher or classmates about what you can do to improve this essay. Write some notes in case you choose to rewrite this paper later.

Edit

Now review your writing for correctness. Look at spelling, punctuation, and grammar. Read and respond to this checklist alone; then exchange papers and ask a classmate to answer these questions:

Questions for Editing	Yes	No
1. Does the writer use vocabulary that is specific and correct? Notes:		
2. Has the writer used past forms correctly? Notes:		
3. Has the writer used cause and result expressions? Notes:		
4. Are there any grammar mistakes that you want to point out? If yes, what should the writer check?		

Correct any mistakes your classmate or teacher pointed out in the Editing Checklist. Now you are ready to place your writing in your Writing Portfolio. You may choose to rewrite it or expand it to a longer piece now or later.

PUTTING IT ALL TOGETHER

◇ **Use What You Have Learned**

Write about another important person or event from the twentieth century. Use what you learned in this chapter to make your writing interesting and correct. Refer to your teacher's or classmate's comments on your first draft. When you are finished, put your writing in your Writing Portfolio.

Test-Taking Tip

Make sure you allow for time at the end of an essay test to check your work. Ask yourself content questions, such as: Did you answer the question? Did you stick to your point of view? Ask yourself organizational questions, such as: Did you answer all parts of the question? Are the paragraphs and sentences logically ordered? And finally, check for any grammar or punctuation problems.

CHECK YOUR PROGRESS

On a scale of 1 to 5, rate how well you have mastered the goals set at the beginning of the chapter:

1 2 3 4 5   write about an important person or event from the twentieth century, state why the person or event is important, and support your statement with specific examples.

1 2 3 4 5   review various past forms, including irregular verbs.

1 2 3 4 5   practice using cause and result expressions in your writing.

1 2 3 4 5   use a variety of sources for supporting information.

If you've given yourself a 3 or lower on any of these goals:

- visit the *Tapestry* web site for additional practice.

- ask your instructor for extra help.

- review the sections of the chapter that you found difficult.

- work with a partner or study group to further your progress.

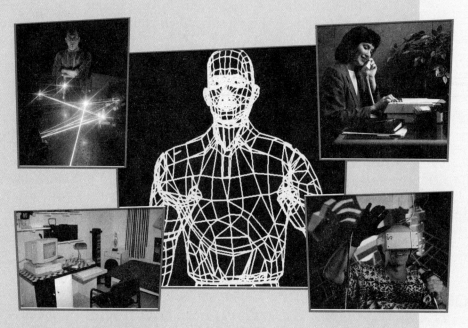

"When the technology is so good that you don't think of it as technology, people adopt it instantly."

—Neil Gershenfeld

Read the quotation by Neil Gershenfeld about technology. What do you think he means? Do you agree? Write down a few of your own ideas about technology:

_____

_____

_____

_____

10

LOOKING FORWARD

We all have hopes for the future. Many people hope for an easier, safer, or more peaceful and prosperous world. What will the future bring? What are the events, inventions, and discoveries of the future? Who will make them? In this chapter, you are going to make predictions about the future.

Setting Goals

In this chapter, you will practice writing a prediction. Specifically, you will predict a future technology. You will also explain how the technology will work, give a scenario, and present the advantages and disadvantages of the technology. In order to do this, you will:

◈ use future expressions to make predictions.

◈ use gerunds to explain how something works.

◈ identify main ideas for reading and writing.

◈ create an outline to organize your ideas before you begin writing.

◈ learn to manage your time.

What additional goals do you have for this chapter? Write them here:

_____

_____

Getting Started

In this chapter, you are going to make a prediction about the future. To get started, answer this question with a partner:

- What do you think the most important invention, discovery, or event of the future will be?

MEETING THE TOPIC

Look at the photos of current technology services and products. Discuss them. What is your opinion of each one? Is it useful? Does it make life easier or harder? Take notes on your discussion.

The Internet

Computer Games

Cell Phone

Personal Digital Assistant

E-Mail

Digital Video Disc Player

Give and get information about technological products and services. First, brainstorm for ones that are common today, but didn't exist when you were a child. Then make a list of any devices you have heard or read about that are being *developed* now and will someday be a part of everyday life. If you can't think of any, guess or use your imagination. What do you *think* will be possible in the near future?

Technological devices that didn't exist when I was a child:

e.g.:   fax machines   cell phones

> The world is so fast that there are days when the person who says it can't be done is interrupted by the person who is doing it.
>
> —ANONYMOUS

Technological devices of tommorrow:

e.g.: wrist phones

Now ask classmates questions about technological devices in their everyday life. Use the following chart. Find out what your classmates use, and their opinion of it. Then ask them what doesn't exist yet but would be a good idea.

Name	Technology I Use	It Makes My Life Easier/Harder	A Better/New Idea
Jhing Wei	laptop computer	easier	

◆**Freewrite**   You've had a chance to look, listen, and talk. Now connect your ideas in writing. Write about one technological product or service you think is possible in the future. Write for ten minutes without stopping. You can write notes or sentences or make a list. Write as quickly as you can. Don't worry about grammar or spelling; just get your ideas on paper.

TUNING IN: "Future Technology"

In this CNN video, you will watch a futurist (an expert on the future) talk about new technology. First, read the following questions. Then watch the video and answer the questions.

© CNN

Future technology

1. Which technology does futurist George Gilder think everyone will have soon?

    a. Smaller cars.

    b. Pocket TVs.

    c. Pocket supercomputers.

2. What kind of communication has increased in recent years, according to Gilder?

    a. Postal mail.

    b. E-mail.

    c. Video conferencing.

3. What is the name of the technology that is improving communication?

    a. Fiber optics.

    b. Chip optics.

    c. Silicon optics.

4. What is one benefit of the changes in information technology?

    a. It gives individuals power.

    b. The home can become a production center.

    c. Both **a** and **b**.

5. What does Gilder say about technology?

    a. It will destroy jobs.

    b. It creates wealth.

    c. It will make people lazy.

EXPANDING YOUR LANGUAGE

Vocabulary Check

Expand your vocabulary by studying some words and expressions that people use to talk about the technology of the future. Check the words you already know. Work in small groups. Add new words to your Vocabulary Log.

_____ complex	_____ simple
_____ gadget	_____ technological
_____ innovation	_____ technology
_____ innovative	_____ to come up with
_____ integrated (with)	_____ to develop
_____ interactive	_____ to invent
_____ invention	_____ to operate
_____ on the market	_____ to simplify
_____ process	_____ to transmit
_____ product	_____ to work
_____ research, researcher	_____ virtual

Vocabulary Tip

Know Parts of Speech

Knowing parts of speech will help you understand how to use new words in writing. Test your knowledge of the parts of speech of some of the words in the Vocabulary Check. Complete the following charts (below and on the next page) with all the forms for the words from the list.

Noun	Verb	Adjective	Adverb
	invent		
process			
technology			
innovation			

Noun	Verb	Adjective	Adverb
	operate		
		simple	
	develop		
		interactive	

Vocabulary Building

A virtual reality (VR) is a three-dimensional computer simulation that provides sensory information (sight, sound, and/or others) to make you feel that you are in a "place." Eventually, VR will be used in high school and college classrooms. Students will be able to work with virtual DNA, explore virtual ecosystems, tour virtual museums, and explore virtual galaxies.

Practice your knowledge of parts of speech. Fill in the blanks in the following sentences with the correct form of the words in parentheses.

1. (develop) Technological _____ have made our lives much easier.

2. (technology) A computer is a _____ device that I cannot live without.

3. (operate) This manual explains the _____ of the machine, but I don't understand it.

4. (simple) The manual is too difficult to understand; I wish computer companies would _____ their instructions.

5. (invent) In my opinion, the best _____ of the twentieth century was the cell phone.

6. (innovation) One of the most _____ things I've seen on the Internet is three-dimensional chat rooms.

7. (process) This computer _____ information slowly because it's so old-fashioned.

8. (interactive) This new computer program lets you _____ with other users around the world.

Now rewrite your freewrite, page 216. Use at least five of the words from the word list. Use any forms of the words that you wish.

Grammar You Can Use: Future Expressions

In this chapter, you are going to make a prediction about a new technology. If you aren't absolutely certain about a new product or invention, you can use *probably* in your statement.

> *will* + *probably* + verb

EXAMPLES:

Sony *will probably develop* smaller CD players in the future.

Some day, you *will probably be able to do* everything online, even go to school.

Another way to show that you are not absolutely certain is to use a modal of probability such as *may* or *might* instead of *will*.

> *may/might* + verb

EXAMPLES:

Sony *might develop* smaller CD players in the future.

Some day, you *may be able to do* everything online, even go to school.

Practice making predictions. Pretend it's 1970. Pick three things you discussed in Meeting the Topic on page 214. These haven't been invented yet. Write a prediction about each one, using *will* + *probably* + verb or *may/might* + verb.

_____

_____

_____

_____

_____

_____

_____

◇ Grammar You Can Use: Using Gerunds to Explain How Something Works

You are also going to explain how something works. One way to do this is to use a gerund (verb + *ing*).

> (a product or service)   *works/operates* + *by* + verb + *ing*

Look at these examples:

- The electric garage door opener *operates* simply *by pushing* a button.

- Mobile phones *work by having* a transmitter placed every few miles.

1. Practice explaining how things work using this form. Write five sentences explaining how the objects work that you discussed in Meeting the Topic (page 214).

_____

_____

_____

_____

_____

2. Now rewrite your freewrite assignment using at least one X *works by verb + ing* form.

READING FOR WRITING

One of the best ways to improve your writing is to read other people's work. Through reading models, you can get ideas about the topic and learn how other writers predict future products. You are going to read a short magazine article called "Virtual Hospitals." The second is an article called "Smart TV."

Getting Ready to Read

Before you read, answer this question:

- What do you think the article will be about, based on the title "Virtual Hospitals"? Think about the meaning of *virtual*.

As you read, answer this question:

- What are some possible advantages of a virtual hospital? What are some disadvantages?

Read

Reading 1: Virtual Hospitals

1 Soon, creating a hospital in cyberspace may no longer be science fiction. NASA's Ames **Research** Center and Salinas Valley Memorial Hospital are working together to bring a **virtual** medical facility to the World Wide Web in the near future.

2 The venture will involve machines that **transmit** and receive data and three-dimensional (3-D) images[1] of the human body via a special workstation located at the hospital. Medical professionals will send diagnostic information[2] to NASA through its **Research** and Education Network, which will **transmit** the 3-D images and data back to the hospital for evaluation and image manipulation.[3] The doctors will then give feedback about how well the network works and the quality of the images.

3 A key aspect of creating and maintaining a practical **virtual** hospital is the ability to send high-quality images in real-time.[4] Using this **technology,** doctors can participate in group training procedures, and even conduct practice operations on a 3-D patient. Future plans for the project call for setting up Internet-based facilities for remote areas and in space with the help of professionals at the Stanford University Medical Center and the Cleveland Clinic.

—Technology News: Virtual Hospitals.

After You Read

1. What is a virtual hospital?

2. How will it work?

3. What are the advantages of a virtual hospital?

4. What are the disadvantages, in your opinion?

Getting Ready to Read

Before you read, answer these questions:

- Do you ever buy things on the Internet? Describe how you do it.

- Do you think buying on the Internet is a good idea? Why or why not?

As you read, answer this question:

- How is this new service like something we already have?

[1]**three-dimensional images:** an image (picture) that has depth as well as height and width

[2]**diagnostic information:** information that helps a doctor decide what is wrong with a patient

[3]**image manipulation:** turning a picture around in order to see all sides.

[4]**real-time:** in the present

⬦ Read

Reading 2: Smart TV

1   Hate to shop at the mall? Love to watch TV? See clothes, **gadgets,** or furniture on your favorite TV shows that you would just love to have? Lots of other people feel the same way, apparently, and that's why entertainment companies will soon be selling products that you can buy while you watch TV.

2   "Within the next five years, the Internet will be fully **integrated with** television," explains Laura Buddine, president of the interactive **research** firm IACTA. "And fashion will likely be one of the first areas to feel the impact."

3   Buddine predicts that we will be able to buy products immediately via **interactive** TV programs, or "smart TV" when the Web is **transmitted** through our TV sets. Smart TV will work by just clicking your remote control on the object you desire. For example, you can click on the jeans that the handsome guy is wearing in your favorite sitcom, stop the program, and link to a buying area on a website. Enter in your credit card information and address, and soon the jeans will be at your door, just as with online shopping today. Click again, and resume watching your favorite program.

4   Let's say you're watching a James Bond movie on TV and you see the dapper Bond in a cool tie. Click—"You'll immediately be sent to a **virtual** image of the Savile Row [London, England] shop where the tie is made," says Burckard Hoene, founder of the online Fashion Planet. Hoene is in the **process** of creating a database of the clothes worn in thousands of movies and music videos. "We're going to see a melting pot of industries," says Hoene. "Fashion, Hollywood, and music all working together."

5   Smart TV appeals to the American desire for immediate gratification. But experts say it will be a challenge to do Smart TV right. Americans are already becoming so used to the selling of products on TV that this may not be as appealing as some think. "I think smart shopping will be one of the first applications of **interactive** television," says Geraldine Laybourne, who resigned in 1998 as president of Disney/ABC Cable Networks to **develop** quality Web content for women. "But unless we do it right, we will turn the audience away."

—adapted from "I Want My Smart TV,"
Vogue, December 1998, pp. 144–146.

> **Genetically engineered foods are foods that are "improved" by genes from other plants or animals. This can enhance nutrition, taste, or the length of time the food stays fresh. Depending on public reaction, these foods may be widely available in the future.**

⬦ After You Read

1. What is Smart TV?

2. How will Smart TV work? Does it already exist in some places? How does it work?

3. Would you like to have Smart TV? Why or why not?

4. Do you think Smart TV is a good idea? Why or why not?

LANGUAGE LEARNING STRATEGY

Identify the main idea of a reading passage. It can be a useful example of one way to state a main idea in your own writing. You can improve your writing by stating your main idea clearly.

Apply the Strategy

Where is the main idea stated in "Smart TV"? Underline it. Is it a prediction?

FROM READING TO WRITING

Answer these questions about "Smart TV" to prepare for the writing assignment for this chapter. These exercises use the reading selection to teach you about writing.

1. Look at the first few sentences. Does the reporter get your attention? How?

2. Does the reporter state the main idea of the article? Where is it? Is it a prediction?

3. Does the reporter quote experts? Who are they? Are they good sources, in your opinion? Why do you think she does this?

4. Does the reporter explain how the service will work? How does she do this? Do you understand it?

5. What are the advantages of Smart TV?

6. What are the disadvantages of Smart TV?

7. Which transition word separates the advantage from the disadvantage? Underline it.

◇Getting Ready to Write

Writing to Predict

When you are making a prediction about technology, you grab your readers' attention, state your main idea, give a scenario that explains how the product or technology will work, and summarize the possible advantages and disadvantages of the new technology.

Grab Your Readers' Attention

You want to grab your readers' attention to get them as excited about the new technology as you are. One way to do this is to ask them a question. Ask the question so that their answer will make them understand how important the new technology is. Their answer tells them that there is a need for the product.

EXAMPLES:

- Are you tired of getting junk e-mail?
- Have you ever wanted to play the piano without taking lessons?

Practice Write three attention-grabbing questions for one of the items in Meeting the Topic on page 214.

State Your Main Idea

Your main idea for this kind of writing is your prediction. State it early in your essay, usually at the end of the first paragraph, after you have gotten your readers' attention. You can support your prediction by quoting what experts say. If you use quotations, review the information on quotations in Chapter 8, page 183.

Practice Write three prediction statements about new technology. You can use your ideas from the chart in Meeting the Topic on page 214.

Give a Scenario

One way to show how something works that doesn't exist yet is to use a scenario. To write a scenario, you imagine a typical person using the product or service, and you describe the person's experience. For example, imagine that the cell phone is a new product. Here's a scenario that shows how it works:

Helen no longer has to be in her office to return business calls. Now she can return calls from anywhere. On one busy Monday morning, Helen gets into her car for the long commute to her office. While waiting in traffic, she picks up the cell phone on the seat next to her. It's tiny—it weighs only 6 ounces. She presses a button and connects to her voice mail. She listens to messages from her clients. After each one, all she has to do is press another button, and she immediately connects to the person who left the message. By the time Helen reaches her office, she has returned all her important calls for the day.

Practice Write a scenario for one of the technologies you have already discussed.

Summarize Advantages and Disadvantages

You can conclude your essay by summarizing the advantages and disadvantages of the new product. This can be your opinion or the opinion of experts.

EXAMPLE: The cell phone saves businesspeople time because they can work from their cars while they commute. [Advantage] However, cell phones can be dangerous if they distract people from paying attention to their driving. [Disadvantage]

Notice that you separate advantages from disadvantages with a transition word that shows contrast such as *however* or *but*.

Practice One way to think about the advantages and disadvantages of a new product or service is to make a *pro* (advantage) and *con* (disadvantage) chart. Use the following chart. Complete it with pros and cons of one or more of the products that you discussed in Meeting the Topic. Then write two sentences about the product: one that tells about an advantage and one that tells about a disadvantage. Use a transition word.

Product: _____

Pros	Cons

Choose a Topic

Get into small groups with your classmates. Work as a team to brainstorm for possible new services and products. One way to do this is to think about what already exists and improve on it, as with Smart TV. Then work alone. Choose your own idea to write about.

Plan Your Writing

If you want to discuss something that people are already working on, find background information about your product or service at the library or online. Try science and business magazines. Find experts to quote. Take notes on your research. You can also do research if you want to discuss a new idea: find information on an existing technology and explain how the new one is related to it.

Now design your product or service. Consider how it will work and what it will be used for. You can also decide how it will be made, how big it will be, how much it will weigh, and how much it will cost. Write down your ideas in notes. If possible, draw the product to show how it will look when it is finished.

After you design your product or service, talk about it to your class. Show the drawings. Ask and answer questions about one another's inventions.

Finally, using input from your presentation, make any necessary changes to your product.

LANGUAGE LEARNING STRATEGY

Create an outline to organize your ideas before you begin writing. An outline will help you see if you have included all the important information about your topic. It helps you make changes before you write. It also provides a guide to follow as you write.

Apply the Strategy

Fill in the following chart with information about your product or service:

What need will it fill? (This will help you grab the readers' attention.)
What is it called? What does it look like? (Size? Weight? Similar to another product or service?)
What is it for? How does it work?
What do experts say about it?
What are the advantages and disadvantages of the product or service?

Study an Example

Read this example of a student's essay and answer the questions that follow.

On Cars of the Future

1 Will it become less necessary to go outside in the future? Will driving in the future be less important than it is today because of the development of home entertainment and communication technologies such as the Web and virtual 3-D computer games? The influence of these technologies seems to be keeping us inside our homes. For example, today's children spend more time inside than ever before. However, I don't think future technologies will mean the end of cars. Rather, future technology will influence automobile design.

2 First of all, I think that cars of the future will have the option of being automatic. That is, if conditions warrant it, you will be able to set your car in automatic mode. For example, during rush hour or in bad weather, your car can be completely controlled by a computerized traffic center. That way you can arrive home relaxed and in good shape. However, if you, like many people, love to drive and like being in control, you will have that option, too.

3 Another technological advance in cars will be the use of virtual reality for driver training. Soon, young people will be able to learn how to drive at home or in a computer lab using 3-D virtual software programs that simulate the actual experience of driving a car. This way, they can get realistic training without being dangerous to other drivers.

4 Even though we enjoy many virtual activities that don't require us to leave our homes, driving, cars, and mobility will not disappear. But future cars, like other technologies, will only improve our lives as long as we think about real human needs and uses as we design them.

—Hiroyuki Matsumaru

1. What did you like about this essay?

2. Did the writer choose an interesting topic?

3. Did the writer get your attention? Did he present his main idea clearly? Did he explain clearly how the new technology will work?

4. Do you have any suggestions for Hiroyuki?

ACADEMIC POWER STRATEGY

Learn to manage your time as you move forward in your studies. If you learn how to manage your time now, you will be able to accomplish everything you have to do, meet all your deadlines, and have time leftover for fun. For example, you are going to begin a writing assignment. When will you do it? How long will it take? What other assignments do you have this week? What appointments do you have this week? Do you have time to see your friends and have fun, too?

Apply the Strategy

Plan your week. Include all the things that you have to do and all the things that you want to do. Decide how long things will take and when they are due. Practice this by filling in the following schedule. Then buy an appointment calendar at a drug or stationery store and keep a schedule every week. Follow these steps:

1. Write down the things that you *must* do—for example, classes and appointments—in the correct places.

2. Write down anything that you have to do to prepare for your assignments. Show the days and times that you will prepare.

3. Write the due dates of your assignments in the correct places.

4. Now decide how long it will take you to do each assignment. Then mark the times each day *before* the due date that you will work on the assignments.

5. Write down fun or personal things that you will do in the time that is left over—for example, phone family, go to the movies with friends, go shopping.

| MONTH: _____ YEAR: _____ | | | | | | |
	Monday	Tuesday	Wednesday	Thursday	Friday	Saturday	Sunday
8 A.M.							
9 A.M.							
10 A.M.							
11 A.M.							

	Monday	Tuesday	Wednesday	Thursday	Friday	Saturday	Sunday
12 N							
1 P.M.							
2 P.M.							
3 P.M.							
4 P.M.							
5 P.M.							
6 P.M.							
7 P.M.							
8 P.M.							

 Write

Predict a technological product or service of the future. Write about the invention or product your group designed, or another one.

After You Write

Revise

Now have someone else read your writing so that you know what to add or take away. Remember that in this stage of the writing process, you are looking at ideas. Exchange your paper with a classmate or give your paper to your teacher, your mentor, or a friend to evaluate by answering these questions:

Questions for Revision	Yes	No
1. Does the writer grab your attention at the beginning? Notes:		
2. Does the writer state the main idea clearly? Notes:		

Questions for Revision	Yes	No
3. Does the writer explain how the new product or service works? Notes:		
4. Does the writer discuss the advantages and disadvantages of the product or service? Notes:		

Plan your revision by reading the checklist. Talk with your teacher or classmates about what you can do to improve this essay. Write some notes in case you choose to rewrite this paper later.

Edit

Now review your writing for correctness. Look at spelling, punctuation, and grammar. Read and respond to this checklist alone; then exchange papers and ask a classmate to answer these questions:

Questions for Editing	Yes	No
1. Does the writer use vocabulary that is specific and correct? Notes:		
2. Does the writer use different ways of predicting the future (for example, *may, might, probably*)? Notes:		
3. Does the writer use gerunds to show how the product or service works? Notes:		
4. Are there any grammar mistakes you want to point out? If yes, what should the writer check?		

Correct any mistakes your classmate or teacher pointed out in the Editing Checklist. Now you are ready to place your writing in your Writing Portfolio. You may choose to rewrite it or expand it to a longer piece now or later.

PUTTING IT ALL TOGETHER

◇ **Use What You Have Learned**

Write about another technological innovation. Use what you learned in this chapter to make your writing interesting and correct. Refer to your teacher's or classmate's comments on your first draft. When you are finished, put your writing in your Writing Portfolio.

Test-Taking Tip

If you don't have enough time to finish an essay question on a test, outline the rest of your answer and write a note to your instructor explaining that you ran out of time. By using an outline to show the information that you had planned to include in the essay, you may not get full points, but you will probably get more points than if you left the essay unfinished.

CHECK YOUR PROGRESS

Research is being done on a new kind of security technology which scans the human eye for information that identifies the person. Before long, this technology will take the place of security codes and will be used at bank machines, offices, and other places which require identification.

On a scale of 1 to 5, rate how well you have mastered the goals set at the beginning of the chapter:

1 2 3 4 5   predict a future technology—explain how it will work, give a scenario, and present the advantages and disadvantages of it.

1 2 3 4 5   use future expressions to make predictions.

1 2 3 4 5   use gerunds to explain how something works.

1 2 3 4 5   identify main ideas for reading and writing.

1 2 3 4 5   create an outline to organize your ideas before you begin writing.

1 2 3 4 5   learn to manage your time.

If you've given yourself a 3 or lower on any of these goals:

- visit the *Tapestry* web site for additional practice.
- ask your instructor for extra help.
- review the sections of the chapter that you found difficult.
- work with a partner or study group to further your progress.

SKILLS INDEX

TEXT CREDITS

Pages 40–41: "Aunt June" by Audrey B. Fielding. Printed by permission of the author.

Pages 42–43: Adapted from "Around the Corner" by Sharon Bryan from *In Short: A Collection of Creative Nonfiction,* edited by Kitchen & Jones, W. W. Norton & Co., New York, © 1996.

Pages 66–67 and 68–69: Adapted from "A Confusion of Last Names" and "Why Me?" from *Read: The Magazine for Reading and English,* edited by Hoey, Field Publications, © 1987.

Pages 89–90: Adapted from *The Crosscultural, Language and Academic Development Handbook,* Diaz-Rico and Weed, Allyn & Bacon, © 1995.

Page 91: Adapted from *The Tapestry of Language Learning* by Rebecca Oxford and Robin Scarcella. Copyright © 1992 by Heinle & Heinle Publishers.

Page 113: Excerpt from *A Pilgrim at Tinker Creek,* by Annie Dillard. Harper's Magazine Press, New York, © 1974. Pages 4–5.

Pages 157–158: Adapted from "Delicious Symbolism of Chinese New Year" by Joyce Jue from *The San Francisco Chronicle,* Wednesday, February 5, 1992. Pages F1 & F3.

Page 197: Adapted from "The First Lady's Biography": http://www.whitehouse.gov/WH/EOP/First_Lady/html/HILLARY_Bio.html.1999.

Pages 199–200: Excerpt from "Elvis Presley" by Bunny Gibson from *The Century,* by Peter Jennings and Todd Brewster. Doubleday, a division of Bantam Doubleday Dell Publishing Group Inc., © 1998. Page 344.

Page 222: Adapted from "I Want My Smart TV" by Kristin Zimbalist from *Vogue Magazine,* December 1998. Pages 144–146.

PHOTO CREDITS

p. 2, provided by Meredith Pike-Baky; p. 4, TL Annie Griffiths Belt/Corbis, BL Deborah Davis/PhotoEdit, M Peter Turnley/Corbis, TR Photograph by Jonathan Stark for the Heinle & Heinle Image Resource Bank; BR David Wolff-Young/PhotoEdit; p. 9, provided by Meredith Pike-Baky; p. 11, James Marshall/Corbis; p. 12, Peter Turnley/Corbis; p. 18, BR David Wolff-Young/PhotoEdit; p. 25, Photograph by Jonathan Stark for the Heinle & Heinle Image Resource Bank; p. 30, provided by Meredith Pike-Baky; p. 32, BL Jose Carrillo/PhotoEdit, BR, ML, TM Photographs by Jonathan Stark for the Heinle & Heinle Image Resource Bank; TL Bill Aaron/PhotoEdit; TR Picture Press/Corbis; p. 38, provided by Meredith Pike-Baky; p. 41, provided by Meredith Pike-Baky; p. 43, Genevieve Naylor/Corbis; p. 46, *all* Photographs by Jonathan Stark for the Heinle & Heinle Image Resource Bank; p. 54, provided by Meredith Pike-Baky; pp. 56, 60, Photographs by Jonathan Stark for the Heinle & Heinle Image Resource Bank; p. 63, Bettmann/Corbis; pp. 68, 69, 73, 78, 81, 84, Photographs by Jonathan Stark for the Heinle & Heinle Image Resource Bank; p. 89, Kevin Fleming/Corbis; p. 102, Chase Swift/Corbis; p. 104, TLM, TRM, BLM, BRM, Photographs by Jonathan Stark for the Heinle & Heinle Image Resource Bank, L David Muench/Corbis, R Wolfgang Kaehler/Corbis; p. 112, Stuart Westmorland/Corbis; p. 114, Reuters/Mike Segar/Archive Photos; p. 124, Henry Diltz/Corbis; p. 126, TL Daniel Laine/Corbis, TM Neal Preston/Corbis, TR Neal Preston/Corbis, BL David Allen/Corbis, BM Peter Iovino/Saga/Archive; TR Lynn Goldsmith/Corbis; p. 133, provided by Meredith Pike-Baky; p. 134, Peter Williams/Corbis; p. 141, Neal Preston/Corbis, p. 146, provided by Meredith Pike-Baky; p. 148, L Neil Rabinowitz/Corbis, LM Dave Bartuff/Corbis, LC Jack Moebes/Corbis, RC Patrick Ward/Corbis, RM Jennie Woodcock, Reflections Photolibrary/Corbis, R Stephanie Colasanti/Corbis; p. 152, Kevin Flemming/Corbis; p. 154, 155, Photographs by Jonathan Stark for the Heinle & Heinle Image Resource Bank; p. 170, Bettmann/Corbis; p. 173, BL, BR, TM, TR Bettmann/Corbis, R Fotos International/Archive Photos; p. 191, L Digital Art/Corbis; p. 192, TRM Hulton-Deutsch Collection/Corbis, *all others* Bettmann/Corbis; p. 197, AFP/Hulton-Deutsch Collection/Corbis; p. 199, Bettmann/Corbis; p. 212, TL Lawrence Manning/Corbis, BL Photograph by Jonathan Stark for the Heinle & Heinle Image Resource Bank, TR Walter Hodges/Corbis, BR Roger Ressmeyer/Corbis; p. 214, TL, BR Michael Newman/PhotoEdit, BL Tom McCarthy/PhotoEdit, BM Amy C. Etra/PhotoEdit, TM Bonnie Kamin/PhotoEdit, TR Photograph by Jonathan Stark for the Heinle & Heinle Image Resource Bank; p. 215, L Walter Hodgers/Corbis, R Photograph by Jonathan Stark for the Heinle & Heinle Image Resource Bank.